AMERICA'S HOLLOW GOVERNMENT

How Washington Has Failed the People

AMERICA'S HOLLOW GOVERNMENT

How Washington Has Failed the People

Mark L. Goldstein

BUSINESS ONE IRWIN
Homewood, Illinois 60430

Portions of Chapters 3, 6, and 8 have appeared in
Government Executive magazine.

Sponsoring editor: Jeffrey A. Krames
Project editor: Karen Smith
Production manager: Mary Jo Parke
Designer: Maureen McCutcheon
Jacket designer: Renee Klyczek Nordstrom
Compositor: BookMasters, Inc.
Typeface: 11/13 Palatino
Printer: The Book Press, Inc.

Library of Congress Cataloging-in-Publication Data

Goldstein, Mark L.
   America's hollow government : how Washington has failed the people
/ Mark L. Goldstein.
      p.   cm.
   Includes bibliographical references and index.
   ISBN 1-55623-467-8
   1. Bureaucracy—United States.   2. Civil service—United States.
3. Finance, Public—United States—1933-   I. Title.
JK421.G6   1992
320.973—dc20   91–43820

Printed in the United States of America
1 2 3 4 5 6 7 8 9 BP 0 9 8 7 6 5 4 3 2

For Becky

For Thy Sweet Love Remember'd
    Such Wealth Brings
That Then I Scorn to Change
    My State with Kings.

> —William Shakespeare,
> *29th Sonnet*

A Government Ill Executed,
  Whatever It May Be in Theory,
  Must Be, in Practice, a Bad Government.

—Alexander Hamilton,
The Federalist, No. 70

Preface

We Americans have a peculiar love-hate relationship with government.

We look to Washington to assure equal access to housing and jobs; to establish a minimum wage and create safe working conditions in factories and on farms; to clean pollution from the air and water; to keep families and property safe from foreign armies and domestic criminals; and to provide a financial safety net for the poor, the sick, and the aged.

Yet widespread federal intervention on our behalf is a relatively recent phenomenon. As a people we have never truly—never fully—trusted government. Indeed, in the late 18th century, so powerful was the fear that the Constitution of 1789 would become a blueprint for tyranny that its ratification was assured only after agreement on a Bill of Rights limiting the reach of the national government.

Today, that suspicion of government persists. Problems have seemed to be everywhere in the past decade—a federal deficit seemingly incapable of being controlled, financial fraud at the Department of Housing and Urban Development, tax dollars wasted on over-priced Defense Department purchases, and bribery at the Food and Drug Administration.

When it comes to government, Americans now are apt to tune out. Opinion polls proclaim that people in the United States read less, vote less, and know less about politics and government, civics and history, than ever before. An increasingly disengaged public, fed by a news media largely devoted to controversy and scandal, cares little about, and thinks even less of, its government.

As a result, Americans distant from their government attach little importance to the running of their Constitution. From government they *demand* more, but rarely are they willing to *give* more. They want the benefits Washington provides but not the costs associated with providing those benefits. They want government's power and protection, but seemingly, not its presence. Do more—but do it with less.

This irreducible dichotomy has created America's Hollow Government. Simply stated, we have not invested as much in our government as we have demanded of it. And like anything else plagued by inadequate investment—such as a car pushed too far without an oil change—our government has broken down. Agencies of the largest government on earth are forced to limit, even ignore, programs they have legal and ethical obligations to administer. Denied adequate resources to accompany expanded expectations, the agencies of government have seen morale and productivity decline and mismanagement and fraud rise. In turn, the reputation of public service is sullied, and the perception of incompetent government is perpetuated.

This is a book about limits—the limits of taxpayers' endurance with Washington's politics-as-usual, the limits of what Americans can endlessly demand from their government while begrudging the institution, and the limits of what government deprived of adequate resources can accomplish.

This is a book neither "for" nor "against" government in the traditional sense of political philosophy, in the molds of liberalism or conservatism. Periods of active and restrained government will always follow on the heels of each other as the nation veers from the excess of either extreme. Rather, whatever government we have, we should effectively fund. Whatever type of government we demand, we should support, and whatever government we choose, we should respect.

Mark L. Goldstein

Acknowledgments

To name the many people who gave their time and talent to the creation of this book would neither recognize them adequately nor absolve my debt to their generosity. They include civil servants and congressional staffers, cabinet secretaries and agency administrators, journalists, academics and lobbyists—scores of people who participate in, analyze, and care about American government and public policy.

Still, several individuals deserve special acknowledgment, for without their assistance, *America's Hollow Government* would have remained just wishful thinking. They include John S. McClenahen, who offered suggestions and patiently reviewed the manuscript; Timothy B. Clark, whose ideas, knowledge of government, and support for the project proved invaluable; and my wife, Becky Sherblom, who repeatedly read drafts of the manuscript and made suggestions, and who encouraged me during those times I couldn't bear writing another word.

My parents provided the faith and encouragement that every first-time author deserves; the George Washington University Department of Public Administration faculty were supportive and granted me a leave of absence from my studies; and John Keats, my former journalism professor, showed me the way.

Credit also goes to Charles A. Bowsher, Comptroller General of the United States, whose 1988 James E. Webb lecture to the National Academy of Public Administration, "An Emerging Crisis: The Disinvestment of Government," encouraged my thesis.

Jeff Krames, executive editor of Business One Irwin, and his staff were always helpful. Their suggestions for polishing my prose made a difference in my work.

None of these people, however, are responsible for the content or opinions in this book. Errors by omission or commission, mistakes of fact or interpretation, are mine alone.

M. L. G.

Contents

Introduction

It was a fading soldier's final salute. Dwight David Eisenhower, who for eight years had been president through prosperity and peace, through a self-absorbed complacency the nation had not seen since Calvin Coolidge and Herbert Hoover lived in the White House, sent his final State of the Union message to Congress on January 12, 1961. He followed a tradition as old as the Republic, a musty presidential subservience crafted as part of the Constitution of the United States in the days when the idea of a presidency—let alone a powerful one—had the Founding Fathers arguing for weeks.

Eisenhower's last report on the State of the Union was, befittingly, a review of his years as president. This message was not a call for bold action, but rather a final opportunity to savor success, to sum up. No history books would memorialize its themes; no students would quote his words. Presented only days before the president's more memorable words warning against the dangers of the military-industrial complex, the State of the Union address carried little wisdom and no advice. It was to be all but forgotten in the whirl of the inaugural that was soon to follow. Yet the old general did something that, while quite unremarkable, appears surprising three decades later: He thanked, and paid tribute to, the hundreds of thousands of civil servants who had implemented the policies of his two-term administration.[1]

THE KENNEDY ERA

Eight days and a generation of leadership later, John Fitzgerald Kennedy placed his hand on a family Bible, swore a 35-word oath, and began his tragic trip to martyrdom. His was to be a presidency like no other, comprised, as author David Halberstam has phrased it, of "the best and the brightest."

Even before the 1960 election, in the summer heat of the party conventions, the national press was speculating about the sweeping changes a Kennedy administration would bring. Compared to the government under Eisenhower, "a role grown somewhat passive," it would be transformed to "a role of action in very many fields."[2] What the old general was to Hoover, the press proclaimed, Kennedy was to the early Franklin Delano Roosevelt. "It was 1933 when anything comparable occurred. A New Deal then took over Washington. . . . A Kennedy Administration would be a 'Young Deal'—one run by young people with new ideas and ambitious policies. A new generation of political leaders is seen coming into power."[3]

It was the image and the words, their stark contrast with the past, that made the difference. Kennedy was a handsome and articulate politician; at 43 he was the youngest elected American president. Kennedy was replacing a grandfatherly figure who eschewed the rawest parts of power and politics, an aging hero of a war 16 years past, a conflict not fought by Americans coming of age in 1960. Young Ivy League professors with ideas to increase spending and transform government were to take over as White House advisers. They were to succeed older, conservative businessmen who were more or less content with a world that had not yet embraced the Beatles or accepted perennial deficit spending.

Kennedy's inaugural challenge, an icon since subsumed by cultural camp, required an activist government. In order to "pay any price, bear any burden, meet any hardship," the nation would have to turn its focus from business back to government. Indeed, Americans would be challenged to join in an "historic effort" that boldly asked them what they could do for their country.[4]

Three decades later, there is no denying that Kennedy's words, his vision, and his image, went forth from that time and place. Combined, they excited Americans about the possibilities the government would present—specifically the roles they could play in helping the government solve the problems of people in need at home and abroad. The Peace Corps, for example, became a beacon to the idealistic young, an unequaled chance for them to serve their country and the economically neediest nations at the same time.

The high caliber of Kennedy's advisers and cabinet helped to convince the would-be federal workers that the new president meant his idealistic words—and would act on them. Indeed, David Halberstam, in *The Best and the Brightest*, wrote that the Kennedy men "carried with them an exciting sense of American elitism, a sense that the best men had been summoned forth from the country to harness this dream to a new American nationalism. . . . It was heady stuff, defining the American dream and giving it a new sense of purpose, taking American life, which had grown too materialistic and complacent, and giving it a new and grander mission."[5]

End of the Vision

The idealism, the bold ventures, provided people entering government, and those already part of public service, with a sense of mission Americans don't frequently associate with bureaucracy. Rarely have the goals of government excited ordinary citizens enough that they would answer a politician's call.

It was not to last. Kennedy's magnetism and vision died with him. And since then, Americans have not sought to define themselves and their time through government. That which excited young people in the 1960s must seem quaint, even misguided, to those coming of age a generation later.

By 1965, America was getting mixed signals: Lyndon Johnson's Great Society programs kept an idealistic spark alive even as the expanding war in Vietnam began to extinguish the flame. But the emphasis on public service, on government as a positive force in society, was crowded out by demands of war and civil rights.

THE NIXON ADMINISTRATION

And by 1968, attitudes about almost everything were changing and being challenged. Richard Nixon shrugged off his self-imposed exile and was elected president in a nation shaken by the growing domestic unrest and violence, a nation disheartened by the parade of caskets returning from Southeast Asia.

Nixon brought to the Oval Office a moderate Republican's view of Washington's power, one which held that the country was "approaching the limits of what government alone can do."[6] Yet his was an agenda that became, for a Republican, surprisingly full of social action. Prodded by an activist Congress, and confronted by rising citizen concern over such issues as environmental protection and consumer safety, Nixon signed off on much of the regulatory agenda that, a decade later, leaders of the new Right would decry for its intrusiveness on American business.

The Downfall of Nixon's Presidency

Only later, perhaps too late, did the nation learn that Nixon's presidency was also marked by a profound paranoia—a mistrust of all who did not and would not share his views. There were the legendary White House enemies list—the reporters and politicians who were *persona non grata*—and a supposedly left-leaning civil service he suspected of blocking administration programs. Indeed, Nixon held Eisenhower responsible for not having cleaned the Democrats from the bureaucracy after 20 years of Roosevelt and Truman.

Significantly, this distrust of the civil service led Nixon to begin a process that, with the aid of succeeding presidents, not only tilted the power structure of the executive branch toward the White House, but also altered Americans' attitudes about the federal government and the people who worked in its long corridors of power. It was in the Nixon years that the growth of government programs truly acquired their questionable reputation, as Americans objected to the mixed results and monstrous bills coming due for the policies of the 1960s.

Increasingly, bureaucrats who managed the policies created by Congress and the president were blamed for the government's growth and its problems. John Ehrlichman, an assistant to the president who later went to jail for Watergate-related crimes, saw an us-versus-them mentality between the White House and the civil service that he described to Congress as *guerilla warfare.*[7]

As for Nixon, there seemed to be hardly a public statement the president made about government that didn't blast the bureaucracy. Government, Nixon said during his unprecedented efforts to restructure the executive branch in order to gain more control over it, was "too often unresponsive both to the people whom it exists to serve and to the Presidents whom the people elected to administer it. . . . Americans are fed up with wasteful, musclebound government in Washington."[8]

Creation of a New Bureaucracy

Ironically, in their effort to scale back and control the bureaucracy, Nixon and his White House guard tried to create another bureaucracy, what presidential scholar Richard Nathan later called the *counter-bureaucracy*.[9] By aggressively using the National Security council, a revitalized and renamed Bureau of the Budget, and other councils in the White House, Nixon tried to counteract the agency bureaucrats who developed regulations and carried out the government's programs. Nixon also attempted to reorganize the executive branch with the clear goal of undermining the traditional relationships that existed between the large departments such as Agriculture, Labor, and Commerce, their constituents, and their Capitol Hill overseers. Nixon's obsession with supposed bureaucratic intransigence led him to propose four "Super Cabinet" agencies to replace the existing structure.

Nixon's formal proposal to consolidate government agencies was a product of the Ash Council, the president's handpicked task force on government reorganization. While Congress rejected the super agencies (powerful committee heads had little interest in relinquishing their jurisdiction over departments), it gave a more positive reception to other Ash Council recommendations. Principal among them was the reorganization of the Bureau of the Budget into the Office of Management and Budget (OMB), and the elevation of the agency and its director in the hierarchy of the executive branch. Significantly, as Harold Seidman and Robert Gilmour, experts on government management and organization have observed, approval of the OMB reorganization was historic, a turning point in the concentration of executive branch power within the hands of the president and his personal staff. In seeking to more firmly control the power of government, and by so doing reduce the bureaucracy's ability to function independently, the reorganization "aimed at nothing less than a fundamental change in the balance of power within the federal system."[10]

THANKS TO NIXON

Both Jimmy Carter and Ronald Reagan had Nixon to thank for preparing their ways; both presidents would further strengthen the power of the White House over the civil service. They symbolized the anti-establishment populism that increasingly held sway in the electorate after Vietnam and Watergate. After Nixon, no hint remained of the government's beneficence. Carter and Reagan claimed to hate big government, and denigrated the bureaucrats who made it work. Absent in their attacks was any appreciation of the professional skill and institutional memory needed to keep programs and vital services running while presidents come and go.

Carter, the Outsider

Carter, of course, was the consummate outsider. A clear advantage in the beginning, this quality proved to be just as much a disadvantage in the end. Carter's ignorance of Washington's ways would isolate him from his own party leaders in Congress, and would frustrate his efforts to control the executive branch. Indeed, Carter himself, in his presidential memoirs, *Keeping Faith*, recognized this weakness, and said of his administration: "We came to Washington as outsiders and never appreciably changed this status."[11]

Significantly, the Democrats' brief return to the center of the political stage in the late 1970s was nothing like their activist approach in the 1960s. It is ironic that Carter, in moving into the historic rooms where Watergate had so recently gone awry, had a vision of government more akin to Nixon than to Kennedy.

Nixon, in his second inaugural address, had declared that he offered "no promise of a purely governmental solution for every problem. We have lived too long with that false promise." His words were echoed just four years later in Carter's inaugural address: "We have learned that more is not necessarily better, that even our great Nation has its recognized limits, and that we can neither answer all questions or solve all problems."[12]

Carter shared Nixon's views of the bureaucracy. Part of Carter's attractiveness lay in his ability, as an outsider, to attack Washington's real and imagined excesses, the rising federal budget deficits, and a government supposedly run amok. Whether his relative inexperience in national public policy issues constrained Carter to such safer topics as bashing the bureaucracy, or that he really spoke true to the nation's growing angst, is not important. What matters is that a man elected to this country's highest office for the first time in this century got there by campaigning on the backs of the people who ultimately must administer his policies.

Hostility toward the Government

On the New Hampshire campaign trail, Carter had warned, "Don't vote for me unless you want to see the executive branch of government completely reorganized."[13] It was this hostility toward the civil service, the dark antipathy for government, that Carter voiced time and time again. It was very much in evidence both in the beginning and near the end of his presidency. "We have begun to reorganize and get control of the bureaucracy," Carter boasted in his 1979 State of the Union address.[14]

Carter advanced one step further the White House's administrative control of the government begun by Nixon. Railing against big government, Carter instituted a regulatory review process at the White House that forced bureaucrats to more carefully consider the economic impact of their proposals. In doing so, Carter expanded Nixon's concept of the "counter-bureaucracy," creating in a regulatory analysis review group the powers to reject regulations and to second-guess the professional judgments of civil servants. Modest as these new procedures seemed, their very existence set the stage for the vast changes that would occur when Ronald Reagan moved into the Oval Office.

Carter was often criticized for his focus on the process of government to the detriment of product, and stymied his own policies for lack of clear objectives. According to Seidman and Gilmour, "President Carter's approach to government reorganization was not bold or comprehensive."[15] In fact, elements of Carter's reorganization program had little unifying theme, and certainly none of the vision that as a candidate he had tried to sell to the voters. His attempts to control the bureaucracy were essentially a failure, Seidman says.

Decline of Government Morale

The only lasting impact of Carter's polemics was on the public service itself. The Carter years marked a decisive shift in the views of presidents and the public toward the government and federal workers, and of the bureaucrats toward their own worth and the positions they held. Attacked by the man who nominally had come to lead them, government workers experienced a decline in morale from which they have never recovered. A civil service once proud and energized was abused to further political purposes. Indeed, studies of the federal work force found a civil service stung by the simplistic populism that blamed them for the country's ills. Beginning with Carter, the polls showed that the public servants were increasingly demoralized and dissatisfied with their jobs.

THE RISE OF REAGAN'S POPULARITY

This populism was even more potent in 1980. A national discontent became a dynamic force in the hands of Ronald Reagan. Here was a man whose acting experience made him comfortable with broad themes and large audiences. Reagan captured the country's attention, and its highest office, with his folksy style and simple messages.

In Ronald Reagan, Americans elected a president for whom issues were black and white, yes or no, good or bad. High taxes were bad. The Soviets were evil. Patriotism and a return to simple values were good. And when it came to government, Reagan vowed over and over again to get it "off the backs of the people."

The Reagan Revolution

Reagan ultimately failed in returning government to some mythical past, some grand rollback to the days before the Great Society. In fact, he never truly started the task. As his first budget director, David Stockman, quickly recognized, the Reagan Revolution imploded when the president's advisers failed to push for massive cuts to the government entitlement programs.[16] The one-time head of the Screen Actors Guild had promised, like Carter, to cut the size of government. Along with cutting funds and staff for many programs, Reagan had hoped to sell off profitable chunks of the federal structure to private sector entrepreneurs, in whose hands, presumably, such enterprises could be more efficiently managed. But Congress blocked much of this agenda, and the White House was eventually distracted by scandals and the struggles of a lame duck, increasingly disengaged, president.

Still, Reagan's barrage on the bureaucracy and big government was furious. On Day One of the Reagan Revolution, the newly sworn president stated: "It is time to check and reverse the growth of government, which shows signs of having grown beyond the consent of the governed. It is my intention to curb the size and influence of the Federal establishment and to demand recognition of the distinction between the powers granted to the Federal Government and those reserved to the States or to the people."[17]

Reagan viewed government not only as a threat to American traditions, especially individual freedom, but also as a significant source of the country's economic, social, and psychological ills. "It is no coincidence that our present troubles parallel and are proportionate to the intervention and intrusion in our lives that result from unnecessary and excessive growth of government," he concluded in his 1981 inaugural address.[18]

On that same day, Reagan fulfilled a campaign promise he had made the previous summer. He imposed a strict hiring freeze on the executive branch. Bitterly opposed by a civil service already unable to meet the nation's growing demands on the government, the freeze, Reagan said, was "a first step towards controlling the growth and size of government and stopping the drain on the economy by the public sector. Imposing a freeze now can eventually lead to a significant reduction in the size of the Federal work force."[19]

Reagan's disregard for the professional civil service and the government it managed never wavered. And it was replicated among White House aides. They placed loyal acceptance of the president's philosophy ahead of competency in choosing proven conservatives to lead many agencies. Bureaucrats throughout the government quickly found themselves cut off from power and policy, their professional advice unheeded by the political hierarchy.

Cutting of Personnel and Programs

Probably no president since Franklin Roosevelt had succeeded as Reagan did in consolidating the power of the White House over the bureaucracy. Legions of Reagan loyalists marched into cabinet departments to impose conservative ideology on federal policies and programs. Orders from the president gave OMB power to review and return to agencies all regulations that, basically, it disliked. An elaborate set of cabinet councils worked hard to ensure that new policies contained the conservative imprimatur, and to guard against the president's cabinet being swayed by the bureaucrats who worked for them. The government's personnel office denigrated the civil service and thwarted the career development of the government's senior executives. And OMB, with the help of agency political appointees and a Congress under pressure to resolve the growing deficit, began to cut the personnel and programs that constituted the Democrats' domestic legacy.

Reagan won when it came to cutting the civil service in numerous domestic agencies ranging from the Internal Revenue Service to the Social Security Administration. Reagan also succeeded in creating the largest peacetime military buildup in the nation's history. However, the Pentagon's growth offset the decline in domestic agency personnel, and effectively doomed Reagan's promise to leave behind a smaller government. Ironically, when the rapid growth of private sector contracting to the federal government during the 1980s is factored into agency personnel levels, it can reasonably be argued that Reagan did more to fuel the growth of government than any recent president.

Neither the sting of the criticism nor the extent of domestic agency cutbacks was lost on the bureaucracy. The morale and respectability of the civil service, chiseled away by Carter, were shattered by Reagan. Experienced senior executives left government as the Reagan philosophy was put into practice; and people throughout the country, at all levels of experience and education, chose not to seek public sector employment.

And so government had come full circle in 30 years—Kennedy to Reagan. As the problem instead of the solution, government had fallen backward instead of reaching forward. The nation's best and brightest have sought private sector jobs rather than public service fulfillment. And government itself focuses more on the past, by paying for yesterday's expenses, than on the future and on tomorrow's investment.

BUSH'S PRESIDENCY

With George Bush's election to the presidency, a decade of leadership by outsiders finally ended. Bush has been a federal bureaucrat most of his adult life, and seems to recognize the importance of the civil service in the smooth operation of the government. He at least gives lip service to the idea: Bush appointed as government personnel director, Constance Berry Newman, a woman who started her government career as a secretary and, thus, has firsthand experience with the issues of public service. One of the first speeches Bush gave after his inauguration was to the Senior Executive Service, the cadre of the government's highest ranking career employees. No president had ever addressed this group—at least no formal record exists of such an encounter.

During his first week in office, Bush also met with the President's Council for Integrity and Efficiency, a panel of the government's appointed inspectors general, the agency watchdogs responsible for eliminating waste, fraud, and abuse. Inspectors general had been around the halls of government since 1978, but neither Carter nor Reagan, both so intent on railing against the evils of wasteful government, had ever met with them.

Bush's kind words and evident concern, even the lack of constant criticism, have helped to shore up the bureaucracy's esteem. But the ruin of public service cannot be rebuilt overnight. Twenty years of demoralization and declining working conditions cannot be overcome so quickly. Bush is surely not Reagan—he has proven himself to be a moderate Republican. Yet, there is unlikely to be any reversal of our current age of austerity. Republicans, even many Democrats, are today extremely wary of funding new programs that exacerbate the federal deficit. Years after Reagan's Revolution failed, its spirit still constrains the start or expansion of most federal programs.

Government still doesn't seem to be the answer. Any attempts to fill in the hollows of our government, or provide the government with adequate resources and modern equipment to offset its growing responsibilities, will be hampered by the deficit's continued squeeze on domestic spending. And Congress, controlled by Democrats eyeing a White House long denied them, is not much inclined to champion bigger government—even where it is needed.

For the foreseeable future, then, the ghosts of the populist presidents will still haunt the White House, Congress, and the nation.

THE PEOPLE'S PURSE

When histories are written about modern America, about the rise and struggles of a powerful nation in the final two-thirds of the 20th century, there will be little mention of the country's hollow government. Unlike wars, dissimilar to depressions and presidents, the hollowing of the federal government has occurred as no single, noteworthy event. With no pictures of political conventions, no wrenching descriptions of bread lines, no apparent connection to the American experience, it becomes tougher to point fingers.

America's hollow government has developed slowly over the years, behind the headlines. Though presidential belittling of the bureaucracy has been primarily a phenomenon of the past 20 years, and Reagan's cuts came in the last 10 years, as a nation we have been chipping away at the federal structure for about 60 years. It has been little noticed until recently, as the foundation grew more unstable, and as the consequences of our actions grew more evident.

Hollow government results from the generally unintended and unforeseeable consequences of laws and policies, of parochial interests better known as politics, and of the ignorance and ambivalence of the electorate. Even the Constitution is to blame, as its musty machinery, designed for a slower age, hampers resolute and rapid action by the federal government.

Part I examines the causes of hollow government. Chapter One, "Going Broke," explores the long-term budgetary and structural factors in the government's decline. For it is in the increasing scarcity of tax dollars, and their control by politicians and bureaucrats, that this story is born.

Chapter Two, "Reagan's Republic," examines Ronald Reagan's ideology and his administration's impact on government resources and services. Through tax cuts and a military buildup, budget cuts, and a regulatory clampdown, Reagan altered for a decade or more both the significance and stature of the federal government and its civil servants.

Chapter Three, "The Capitol Circus," looks at the legislative branch. Congress, in its tug-of-war with presidents and the thousands of bureaucrats who manage government programs, employs an agenda all its own: bring home the goods and get reelected. Congress's emphasis on style and pork over substance and oversight, have contributed to America's Hollow Government.

Chapter One

Going Broke

A fter 34 years as a secretary for the Vermont law firm of Stickney, Sargent and Chase, 65-year-old Ida May Fuller stopped into the Rutland Social Security office shortly after she retired in November 1939. A resident of Brattleboro, Vermont, Fuller had gone to Rutland on an errand and decided to inquire about Social Security.

"It wasn't that I expected anything, mind you, but I knew I'd been paying for something called Social Security and I wanted to ask the people in Rutland about it," Fuller later recalled.[1]

A clerk in the office suggested that she fill out a claims form while she was there, and in January 1940 Fuller received the first monthly check paid by the Social Security system. The check was for $22.54, some $2.21 less than she had paid into the program in the three years before her retirement.[2] The federal government, and the demands that Americans place on it, have never been the same since.

Fuller had no reason to think that her simple act—accepting money from the government—would be the first step in the government's 50-year slide to long-term deficit. Yet it was from this innocent beginning that the world's largest welfare state was created. A solitary check in 1940 for $22.54 by the year 2000 will have grown to $250 billion, an enormous check-writing scheme paying cash benefits to 45 million Americans every month.[3]

THE LARGEST WELFARE STATE— SOCIAL SECURITY

Once started in the years of the Great Depression, there seemed no stopping the welfare state's benefit programs. Indeed, direct payments to individuals today soak up more than

41 percent of the government's annual budget. Virtually all such programs began small, then grew as benefit coverage expanded, and as the number of people eligible for entitlements increased over the years. There was no going back once checks for individual citizens began arriving in the mail or at a local government office. Which voters would seek to deny themselves the additional income? Which politician would be brave enough to propose eliminating benefits?

The Growth of Social Security

Four years after Congress passed the original, somewhat limited Social Security law in 1935, it added benefits for survivors and dependents, and expanded coverage for workers above age 65. In 1950, all regularly employed citizens were included in Social Security, along with civilian government workers not covered by the federal retirement system. In 1954, all self-employed farmers and professionals, except attorneys and physicians, were added. Americans employed by foreign governments were added in 1960, physicians in 1965, and members of the clergy in 1967.

Just two decades after Fuller began receiving her monthly checks, Social Security was completely entrenched and the national retirement program already was reaching beyond what creators originally envisioned as a supplementary pension support. Disability benefits were added in 1956, and health insurance was adopted in 1965.

Conceived as financial shelter from the depression's storm, Social Security now sends checks to more than 90 percent of all American workers or their dependents at some point during their lives.[4] About 94 percent of U.S. workers now contribute to the program, insuring disability protection and survivor benefits along with retirement income. Retired Americans and their families account for more than 70 percent of the Social Security recipients, with some 60 percent of the elderly counting on the monthly check to cover at least half of their total cash income.[5] More than 63,000 federal workers are employed to administer a program that sends 468 million checks to beneficiaries throughout the country and around the globe. Depression's storm is long over, but the shelter grows ever larger.

Welfare State Entitlements

Social Security has, over time, become the foundation of our modern welfare state, with the nation subsequently stacking all sorts of other programs atop it in an effort to help Americans avoid hardship and poverty. Among them are food stamps, Medicare, unemployment insurance, farmers' loans and crop subsidies, guaranteed student loans, and veterans' benefits. Called *entitlements* because all Americans who meet set eligibility requirements are entitled to receive benefits until Congress changes the law, social welfare and insurance programs make up the largest—and still growing—part of funds the government spends every year. This so-called mandatory spending has increased from 28 percent of the budget when John F. Kennedy was president to more than 52 percent during George Bush's administration.[6] The young and the old, the poor and the homeless, families without fathers (all of these, and many more), are the beneficiaries of a system that, in less than a single lifetime, has come to dominate the purse and the purpose of our federal system.

A MISERLY PAST

Our forefathers would surely not recognize today's government largesse. The domestic tranquility they wanted to ensure had little to do with public handouts. America was a land of vast resources, yet the instinct of many early leaders, including Jefferson, Madison, and Monroe, was to limit public spending, and through it, the power of the central government. Capital employed by government was simply capital unavailable for more beneficial commercial interests, a viewpoint not uncommon today, but nearly universal two centuries ago. The wisdom of the founders called for budget surpluses, when they existed, to be used for paying debts. Spending, many of the early leaders said, was the states' domain, so that it could be controlled by the people. Indeed, a parade of presidents lasting until the Civil War was mightily afraid to dig into the public purse, insistent that no spending spree, with its attendant immoral debt and heavy taxes, be started on their watch.

The Republic in its early days was funded almost exclusively through stiff customs duties and the sale of public land to private citizens. Debts from the American Revolution and the War of 1812 were retired quickly because revenues in most years generously exceeded expenditures, allowing the Treasury to apply the surplus to debt reduction. In fact, the coffers were so flush that by 1826 a U.S. Senate committee complained of "the serious inconvenience of an overflowing treasury."[7] (Washington would surely love such inconvenience today!) Even the Civil War, which at its peak in 1865 produced a $2.8 billion public debt (and the nation's first income tax), saw its burden substantially lifted within a few years.[8]

With few exceptions, the government spent nearly half of all its revenues to pay for the Army and Navy during the first 75 years of the nation's existence.[9] Outlays to meet civilian needs, such as improvements to America's roads, bridges, and docks to support commerce, came slowly. Jefferson, ever skeptical of consolidated power, used an early peace dividend from military spending cutbacks to pay down the public debt. Only then was he inclined to devote surplus resources to internal improvements—though he was so uncertain as to the validity of such spending that he urged a constitutional amendment to dispel any doubts.[10]

The Government's Growth

By the time of the Jackson administration, however, the growth of government, in dollar terms, was unmistakable. Federal expenditures which had totaled just $10.8 million in 1800 were some 50 percent larger by 1825. The government then more than doubled its expenditures, to $39.5 million, between 1825 and 1850.[11] Domestic spending, while nearly doubling between 1800 and 1825, nearly quadrupled, from $2.7 million to $14 million, between 1825 and 1850, as the nation built its early infrastructure. Then there came a national milestone: the first significant subsidies were offered to the railroads laying tracks toward a Western wilderness. (The railroads also were largely responsible for the initial growth of the federal administrative and regulatory state, which was ushered in by the Interstate Commerce Act of 1887, enacted to settle freight pricing disputes.) And the first grants, in the form of land for educational institutions, were provided to state governments starting in the mid-19th century.

It was the War between the States and its aftermath, however, that truly started the government's growth. Commercial interests multiplied; the industrial sector was developing apace; and money for all manner of capital improvements was sorely needed. The increasing availability of tariff revenues, combined with historic changes in Congress's committee structure, set the stage for higher federal spending.

THE BIRTH OF THE MODERN CONGRESS

In 1865, Congress created an Appropriations Committee to help the Committee on Ways and Means handle a work load greatly increased by the demands of the Civil War. Here was the birth of the modern Congress, the first dispersion through the legislature of authority to tax and spend. This desire for power over the purse would in time lead to even more committees attempting to exercise control over the Treasury, and would eventually frustrate efforts by Congress as a whole, or any single powerful member, to restrain expenditures.

Money politics and interest groups arose soon thereafter, an inevitable byproduct of gradual government centralization, higher postwar spending, and the increasing influence of individual committees and legislators directing public funds toward favored causes. Iron triangles were created, in which politicians, bureaucrats, and interest groups worked their magic on government spending; they perfected the logrolling and pork barreling practices that Congress still enjoys.

The government's role in the country's economy grew through the needs of industrial development and the nation's expansion throughout the American West. Still, the government's role as protector, a social concept embraced by the Europeans in the 1880s, came slowly to the United States. Not until the Great Depression's depths did the country's new leaders determine that different ways of spending public funds were necessary.

THE MODERN WELFARE STATE

The depression changed everything. Tradition was plowed under and, for better or worse, the nation shifted from balancing the budget to balancing the economy. Deficit spending, emergency work programs, a safety net for mortgages—these and other *radical* programs of Franklin Roosevelt's famous 100 days—altered the purpose of government, infusing it with a moral responsibility for the welfare of the nation's people.

Roosevelt had taken on the cause early. In the 1932 elections he was the sole national political leader to ally himself with social insurance. To him, it was clear that the economic wreckage of depression had left the nation little choice. Ideas many considered radical, even un-American, would be employed to return the country to some measure of prosperity and economic productivity.

Where once government's role had been mainly to build roads and dams, to fight wars, and to care for veterans, now its purpose took on a new meaning. Beginning with the New Deal, government was destined to become the nation's bank clerk, forever transferring increasingly large sums of the taxpayers' money from one citizen to another. As Arthur M. Schlesinger Jr. later wrote, FDR's approach constituted a momentous break with the past. "The federal government was at last charged with the obligation to provide its citizens a measure of protection from the hazards and vicissitudes of life."[12]

In the beginning, this obligation wasn't very expensive. In 1940, the year Ida Fuller began receiving her Social Security checks, the government spent $16 million for social insurance and $1.7 billion for all payments to individuals.[13] For the most part, Uncle Sam's checks went to cover veterans' benefits and for unemployment assistance; there was no welfare or Medicare, no food stamps or Head Start. Housing programs were just starting.

Programs grew slowly. Even in 1950, a decade after the first Social Security checks were printed and cashed, only 16 percent of the over-65 population, about 2 million people, had paid into the program long enough to earn benefits.[14] That year Social Security payments by the government totaled $727 million.[15] Aid to Families with Dependent Children (AFDC), which had been launched simultaneously with Social Security, in 1940 served about 372,000 families; still, its growth was inevitable. By 1960, AFDC paid benefits to more than 800,000 families. Eisenhower, though no welfare state enthusiast, in his presidency supported the Democrats' early entitlement programs, even approving modest expansions to the social insurance system.

Social Programs of the 1960s and 1970s

With the election of the Democrats Kennedy and Johnson, Roosevelt's welfare state was transformed from a shelter to a permanent residence. Social programs, which saw their biggest gains in the 1960s and 1970s, greatly expanded the types and duration of federal assistance available to the nation's disadvantaged. John F. Kennedy, campaigning in West Virginia for president, had been profoundly affected by the deplorable conditions of a destitute Appalachia. Reportedly he had read Michael Harrington's 1962 classic, *The Other America*. And by the spring of 1963, Kennedy decided that the time had come for a comprehensive poverty program, one that could pull together many of the country's existing social programs into an effective whole. As James L. Sundquist notes, Kennedy and his advisers were frustrated by the fact that the handful of existing federal programs created to provide housing and to combat unemployment and delinquency had proven inadequate to the task of eradicating the roots of poverty.[16]

Kennedy saw little of his plan take shape before his assassination on November 22, 1963. The torch passed to Lyndon Johnson who, in his first State of the Union address in January 1964, turned up the volume on the antipoverty rhetoric. "This administration today, here and now, declares unconditional war on poverty in America," Johnson told Congress.[17] His words would dispatch billions of dollars in the direction of the poor over the next five years, and into the hands of a support industry that grew to serve their needs. Congress saluted just a few months after Johnson's declaration of War on Poverty, passing the first of many initiatives that, over about 15 years, would sharply increase federal spending on welfare or social programs. With nearly $1 billion, a newly created Office of Equal Opportunity (OEO) sought to attack the many causes of poverty, including illiteracy, joblessness, and inadequate public services for the poor.

Johnson's War on Poverty

Conservatives have long identified Johnson's War on Poverty as the moment when the welfare state broke free from its restraints. Liberals, on the other hand, have never completely gotten over the fact that their expensive programs solved few of the poor's problems. Yet it was the eroding economic conditions that began in the early 1970s, the growing number of disadvantaged, and the shrinking equality of incomes, that made progress appear impossible and doomed the Great Society more than any administrative failures in federal programs.

Although the welfare state has come to be associated with programs for the poor, in reality, the greatest growth in transfer payments supports Medicare and other programs benefiting the nation's massive middle class. Indeed, the OEO's funds paled in comparison with the $20 billion in transfer payments that the government distributed in 1965.[18] The same is true in the 1990s, as the considerable levels of government funds spent for all kinds of social programs become confused with comparatively much smaller expenditures for actual welfare and poverty-related programs.

The pressure to maintain and expand payments to individuals remains great. Indeed, politicians tinker with entitlements at their careers' peril. The notion of disenfranchisement, of Congress taking away something that it has given to citizens, mixes poorly with reelection. Programs created in times of crisis, such as AFDC, or to support specific needs of the population, such as Medicare or federal loans for education, typically find themselves as the baseline (the minimum standard) for which acceptable funding will be measured in all subsequent years. Once established, such programs cannot be ended without alienating the recipients and voters. Once funded, annual additions serve as the following year's baseline, and any deviation is considered by recipients as a reduction in commitment and dollars to be fought against in Congress and at the polls.

This nearly 60-year legacy of transfer payments has not only made eliminating social programs politically untenable, but also resulted in programs begetting other programs. In opening the door to the welfare state, the government has fundamentally raised expectations and encouraged new demands. Recipients commonly consider federal subsidies as a right, not unlike freedom of speech and of religion. Not only will those now receiving benefits expect future payments, but so too will the Americans who eventually find themselves in need—even if under differing circumstances.

THE RUNAWAY YEARS

In much the same way that Eisenhower inherited the original social welfare programs of the New Deal, Republican Richard Nixon in 1969 found himself acceding to a political reality created by Democrats; that is, the responsibility of the government to alleviate economic and social disadvantages. Between 1968 and 1974, in fact, total payments to individuals by the federal government grew from 28 percent of the budget to 44.7 percent.[19]

Nixon campaigned to "improve and streamline" welfare programs and, when elected, took the task of welfare reform seriously.[20] He hired liberal Harvard University professor and poverty expert, Daniel Patrick Moynihan, and attempted through his Family Assistance Plan to rework—quite radically—Johnson's Great Society.

The Entitlement Programs

But, significantly, Nixon hardly changed the system. In fact, this Republican president turned an experimental food stamps project into a huge, permanent part of the entitlement program. In the end, Congress rejected most of Nixon's efforts, and the president wound up with little that was new. Inexorably, the welfare state's costs climbed as ranks of those eligible to receive benefits grew, and as the pressure on Congress to expand existing programs proved irresistible.

From Eisenhower to Nixon, the American welfare state seemed unstoppable, growing from 40 to more than 400 programs.[21] Little else has so influenced government spending to this very day. The choices made and tax dollars spent on entitlements have put enormous pressure on the federal budget and on the workings of Washington itself. And what entitlements took, other programs were forced to give.

When Richard Nixon took office, 48 percent of the fiscal 1969 federal budget was being spent on defense and 30 percent on health, education, and income-related entitlement programs. When Jimmy Carter entered office, after eight years of Republican administrations, the numbers had essentially reversed themselves: in fiscal 1977, roughly 48 percent of the budget was being spent on entitlement programs.[22]

By almost any measure, the dollars and dimensions of the welfare state became an enormous factor in the government expenditures after the mid-1960s. The creation of programs such as Medicare, Supplemental Security Income, Trade Adjustment Assistance, and food stamps further obligated the Treasury's limited resources and increased demands for economic equality.

Likewise, the number of federal grant programs grew from 132 in 1960 to 379 in 1967 and to 539 by 1981, as expenditures increased from $7 billion in 1960, to $15.2 billion in 1967, to $94.8 billion in 1981.[23]

At the same time, Congress amended and expanded existing programs, including Social Security, Unemployment Compensation, and AFDC. Benefits were boosted to offset inflation's relentless erosion of purchasing power, and programs were expanded to make more people eligible for benefits. Outlays for AFDC, for example, grew by more than 150 percent between 1965 and 1972.

Expansion of Other Welfare and Social Service Programs

Other welfare and social service programs also have greatly expanded:

- Project Head Start, the Health and Human Services program providing educational skills for preschool-age children, received $96.1 million in congressional appropriations in 1965, but by 1990 was costing $1.55 billion, even though its enrollment had actually declined.[24]

- In 1965, food stamps served 424,652 people and cost $32.5 million. By 1975, the government was spending $4.4 billion and providing coupons to 17.1 million Americans. A decade later, in 1985, Washington was handing out food stamps to 19.9 million inhabitants at a cost of $10.7 billion. The program had grown to $14.1 billion by 1990, although it served about the same number of citizens as in 1985.[25]

- Even small programs have dug deeper into the Treasury's pockets. Trade Adjustment Assistance, which provides support to workers made jobless as a result of America's crumbling industrial competitiveness, cost $2.7 million in 1975 and served 665 people. It had grown to $62.7 million in 1990 and benefited more than 17,000 dislocated employees.[26]

A troubled American economy also contributed to the overall rapid growth in entitlement outlays. Economic downturns in 1974, 1977, 1979, 1982, and 1991, by reducing wages and throwing employees out of work, enlarged the pool of people eligible for federal benefits. More food stamps were printed and distributed. Income supplements increased. More people received unemployment compensation.

During the depths of the 1991 recession, more Americans were collecting unemployment benefits and food stamps than at any time in the nation's history. Equally significant, Americans increasingly demanded that the government do something, do anything, to ease their economic pain.

The Role of Inflation

Inflation has played a part in the system's relentless demand for funds. As part of the Nixon administration's efforts to "fix" the welfare system, Congress in 1972 linked Social Security benefits to the Labor Department's consumer price index (CPI), one of the country's basic measures of inflation. Previously, Congress regularly voted benefit increases for Social Security recipients, sometimes 15 percent at a clip. But indexing, in an attempt to ensure payments kept pace with the real costs of goods and services, quickly became a nightmare. Just months after Congress acted, the nation entered nearly a decade of economic chaos in which wages stalled and inflation rose. Entitlement demands increased for all sorts of government social welfare programs. The Social Security trust fund was forced to finance benefits as payroll tax revenues proved inadequate to bankroll the system. Indexing caused instant benefit increases for such federal programs as child nutrition, railroad retirement, veterans' pensions, and food stamps.

Finally, changing demographics have reshaped America's social insurance and welfare programs. Beginning in the 1970s, expanding benefits, a growing elderly population, and sky-high medical costs made Medicare, the government's fastest growing entitlement program, a bloated symbol of the runaway welfare state. In 1967, Medicare benefits cost the government $3.2 billion and served nearly 20 million people. By 1990, Medicare cost $105 billion and served 34.3 million Americans.[27] As the country has aged, Social Security has grown. About 31 million recipients received monthly checks in 1990, which will increase to an estimated 45 million in the year 2000.

BRAKING THE WELFARE STATE

After more than a decade of extraordinary growth, the welfare state began to slow. New social programs were created less frequently in the post-Johnson-Nixon entitlement extravaganza.

Beginning in the Carter years and continuing through the Republican Reagan and Bush administrations, social welfare programs overall lost their momentum. Politicians grew increasingly uncomfortable with proposing large social programs as the federal deficit grew, and as the existing programs became ever more entrenched, both in the budget and as part of society's expectations.

Conservative organizations hailed the cuts that Reagan made to entitlements as the start of a long-overdue scale-back of the welfare state. But attention-grabbing budget cuts to a handful of programs in the early 1980s did little more than curtail benefit payments, some temporarily, to thousands of Americans. Even while recognizing the need for social welfare limits, no president, or Congress has summoned the political will necessary to eliminate significant numbers of entitlements. Ten years after Reagan promised to pare government's scope, both the cost and the number of recipients of the welfare state continue to climb.

The reason is simple: The federal government's largest transfer drains have defied most attempts at legislative limitation. Medicaid, the federal-state health assistance program for the poor and indigent elderly, is one example. Congress at various times in the past decade has curbed benefit payments to existing recipients, while at the same time expanding Medicaid's scope, pulling increasing numbers of disadvantaged Americans into a program now threatening to bust budgets at both the national and state level. Medicaid cost federal and state treasuries about $2 billion in 1967. In 1992, the program is expected to consume about $115 billion. Meanwhile, Social

Security, Medicare, unemployment insurance, and food stamps just keep growing, adding costs and benefit recipients onto an already overburdened system.

Reduction of Welfare Programs

To its credit, Congress has attempted to apply some brakes to the welfare state by tightening eligibility requirements for some programs. Moreover, legislators today are more wary of excessive, open-ended spending commitments for entitlements. A new law now prevents Congress from funding new entitlement programs unless offsetting revenues from other parts of the budget can be found, or unless some special method of paying for prospective programs is guaranteed.

Nevertheless, for all the efforts made by Congress and the Reagan administration to reduce federal outlays for payments to individuals, only two of the principal entitlement programs were cut by more than one-third during the Reagan years. Trade Adjustment Assistance and Guaranteed Student Loans, which had grown rapidly during the late 1970s, were cut back as evidence of ineffectiveness and abuse mounted. Other cuts that did take place didn't last. For example, Supplement Security Income declined by 1.2 percent in 1982 but rose 5.7 percent in 1983. Unemployment insurance was cut by more than 15 percent in 1981 and 1982, but in 1983 regained most of its loss.

Action by the American Association of Retired Persons (AARP)

Meanwhile, such programs as Social Security and Medicare have been for the most part immune to cutbacks. These two programs alone represent 60 percent of the bill for the welfare state. Just the threat of higher premiums and benefit rollbacks has been enough to sound the alarm among such recipient representatives as the American Association of Retired Persons (AARP), an enormously powerful organization with 32 million members and a dedicated Washington lobbying staff. In 1990, the group's heavy hand pressured Congress to repeal the Catastrophic Health Care Act, a law that would have required the wealthiest elderly to pay a small premium increase for their health care.

In a move that could signal how tenaciously interest groups intend to fight repeals of the welfare state, AARP also influenced Congress's rejection of the budget summit in October 1990. Some $60 billion in fiscal 1991 domestic spending cuts in the agreement would have come from Medicare programs, a price AARP deemed too high. Letters and calls to Washington from AARP members objecting to the deal eventually helped to doom it.

Yet if legislators are at all serious about eliminating the federal budget deficit, Americans benefiting from Medicare and many other entitlements will undoubtedly be forced to accept rollbacks in their share of the welfare state. The toughest part is yet to come.

SQUEEZING THE REST

The failure of successive administrations and Congresses to control the rapid growth of the welfare state has had lasting consequences, both for government and for the country as a whole. Quite simply, by taking up an ever greater share of the federal budget, increases in entitlements have ultimately meant decreases in the funding of other programs. Often, the result has been a hollow government.

Today, entitlements and interest on the national debt constitute a dominant and growing share of the federal budget. Indeed, by the time America entered the 1990s, nearly two-thirds of all federal spending was the direct result of government obligations to either Uncle Sam's citizens or his lenders. When politicians decry a budget running out of control, these are the big ticket items they have in mind. Entitlements and interest payments constitute most of the uncontrollable portions of the budget, the basically fixed costs of government spending that Congress either cannot easily—or willingly—change.

Laws provide that anyone eligible for benefits, such as Social Security, Medicare, food stamps, and the other programs on the smorgasbord of federal aid, must be paid regardless of whether the government is running a surplus or a debt. The same is true for interest on the debt. The Treasury pays for these past commitments as claims come due, unless Congress specifically directs otherwise.

Thus, the budget's uncontrollable portion simply grows and grows. In fiscal year 1985, 72.9 percent of the budget was "off limits" to congressional appropriators. Just five years later, in fiscal 1990, the spending over which Congress had lost control had increased to 78.4 percent of the total budget.

Domestic Discretionary Funds

As uncontrollable outlays have continued to rise in relation to the total funds Congress approves each year, it has meant less money for the programs legislators *can* control. Hardest hit has been the domestic discretionary budget. Domestic discretionary funds are the fiscal operating base for a whole host of federal agencies—those things that most Americans recognize as the federal government, including the Internal Revenue Service, the National Weather Service, the National Park Service, the Department of Agriculture, and the U.S. Coast Guard. Also included is spending for basic scientific research; investments in roads, bridges, and government buildings; and public health and education. These agencies and programs have grown hollow, as the gap between budgets and demands for services widen.

It is no coincidence that the decline in federal funds available for domestic discretionary spending began after the welfare state claimed ever-larger parts of the federal budget in the 1970s and 1980s. As a result, 1990 spending for federal domestic programs accounted for just 3.8 percent of the country's gross national product. Just a decade earlier, in 1980, nondefense domestic discretionary spending stood at 5.7 percent of GNP, the highest it has been in 30 years.[28] The Congressional Budget Office predicts, unfortunately, that this slice of federal spending will continue to shrink, dropping to about 3.4 percent of GNP by 1995, further limiting spending for critical government services in which demand continues to outstrip resources.

By a different measure, spending for domestic programs has dropped from 24 percent of the budget in 1981 to less than 16 percent today. The federal government now spends only slightly more on these programs than on interest for the national debt, which consumes a staggering 14 percent of the budget.

Consider the following examples of budget pressures:

- If the total $1.2 trillion U.S. budget for fiscal year 1990 had been equal to $1, just 2 cents would have gone to education, and only about a penny would have been spent on all housing programs.[29]
- Funding for economic development and transportation now is about half as large, relative to GNP, as it was during most of the 1970s. And spending for education, training, social services, and medical research currently is only about three-fourths as large as it was in the late 1970s, relative to GNP.[30]
- Figuring depreciation by the same formula that homeowners or businesses use, the federal government's share of net public investment has averaged about zero since the mid-1970s.[31]

Reagan-era cuts have accelerated the governmental decline brought about by the expanding welfare state's continued squeeze on the domestic budget. As a result, agencies throughout Washington are now without the resources to pursue the programs Congress assigned to them or to initiate policies and programs rightly expected of their mandate.

The consequences of inadequate funding—what the government's comptroller general has characterized as disinvestment—has been found in scores of federal agencies. Here are a few examples:

- The Immigration and Naturalization Service has been unable to keep up with the flow of legal, no less illegal, aliens. Border patrol planes are typically old and unsafe, and some can't even be flown. Their physical condition has undercut the nation's ability to monitor and defend its borders. Backlogs and lines at U.S. ports of entry and regional centers, especially in the summer, regularly overwhelm short-handed immigration posts. The agency's investigative units operating inland from the borders to chase down illegal and criminal aliens have been cut back at a time when crime perpetrated by this shadowy segment of society has been on the rise.

- The Internal Revenue Service (IRS) struggles with a rising tide of tax returns. Its ability to audit Americans continues to decline at the same time the amount of taxes owed by individuals and corporations grows. And despite higher budgets and more personnel, IRS productivity plummeted nearly 20 percent during the 1980s, the result of higher work loads, a more complex tax system, and archaic computer systems. Its ability to win big corporate tax cases is desultory: the IRS routinely loses three-quarters of the corporate cases it brings to trial.

- The nation's air traffic system has expanded at a record pace during the past decade, at the same time an underfunded Federal Aviation Administration (FAA) often was unable to meet congressionally mandated hiring targets for its inspectors and controllers. Experienced air traffic controllers are still absent from many control towers a decade after Ronald Reagan broke their union's illegal strike. And although staffing levels have increased, so, too, has the workload. In 1991 the General Accounting Office reported that a 30 percent increase in air traffic since 1981 had been accompanied by a 16 percent *decrease* in fully certified air traffic controllers.[32] Even when controllers were hired, many of these $60,000-a-year traffic cops of the skies wound up doing routine maintenance, inspection, and other jobs because the FAA didn't have enough funds to hire a sufficient number of employees.

- The U.S. Forest Service, faced with staff cuts and a growing number of visitors seeking recreation in the national forests, in 1990 faced a $449 million maintenance backlog—more than twice the amount the agency reported in 1986—that makes many of its facilities unsafe and unusable. This has occurred in large part because the agency has not had enough funds for daily operations; consequently, maintenance and repairs have been a low priority.[33]

THE UNCHARTED BUDGET

The squeeze on federal programs and on the agencies that administer them will get worse. Besides the dwindling budget share destined for domestic discretionary programs, fiscal problems of the future could make today's hollow government seem vigorous and effective. A legacy of long-ignored problems threatens to divert to a series of federal sinkholes hundreds of billions of tax dollars from programs that could improve our social and economic well-being.

Problems of the Commercial and Thrift Institutions

The problems left to fester in the 1980s have infected the federal budget in the 1990s. For example, Uncle Sam's obligation to pay off depositors in insured commercial banks and thrift institutions drains tax dollars from future-oriented programs to remedy past blunders. Including interest on borrowed funds, the Treasury will pay out an estimated $500 billion to resolve the savings and loan (S&L) crisis, hindering the nation's prospects for early relief from its $399 billion annual budget deficit.

Alarmingly, an eerie parallel of the S&L crisis now threatens commercial banks. The Federal Deposit Insurance Corporation (FDIC), which since the Great Depression has used its Bank Insurance Fund to prop up failing commercial banks, is itself on the brink of failing. Increased bank competition in the 1960s and 1970s, combined with deregulation and other changes to the banking industry in the 1980s have endangered an unprecedented number of large commercial banks; many have failed or nearly failed.

In response, the FDIC has been forced from the early 1980s to dip deeper into its insurance funds. Indeed, from 1980 to 1987, the FDIC resolved 631 banks at a cost of more than $10 billion—more than it had done in its entire 47-year existence. During the 1970s, by comparison, the FDIC resolved 76 commercial bank failures at a cost of $110 million.[34]

The real estate crash and economic recession of 1990 and 1991 further accelerated the insurance fund's depletion as more banks failed, prompting the then FDIC chairman, L. William Seidman, to warn that the unexpected loss of one or more large money-center banks could wipe out his independent government agency altogether. The 1991 failure of one of the Northeast's largest banks, Bank of New England, reduced the bank fund to less than $4 billion. Indeed, the FDIC has been forced to regularly revise the number of commercial banks it expects to fail by the end of 1992. In May 1991, the FDIC estimated some 330 commercial banks would fail. Just one month later, in June 1991, the bank regulator was expecting some 440 banks to expire.

The bank fund's flirtation with insolvency could require a bailout either from the federal Treasury or in the form of higher premiums from an already shaky commercial banking industry. A concerned Congress already has greatly increased the FDIC's borrowing authority in an attempt to avoid another costly bailout of the banks, this time on the eve of national elections. Though the FDIC, as a government corporation, does not show up in the normal accounting for the federal budget, its dwindling reserves do matter when it comes to reducing the deficit. When the FDIC borrows from the Federal Financing Bank, a Treasury Department unit, government bonds are sold to raise the cash requested by the agency, thus increasing the nation's debt and the annual interest costs necessary to service the debt.

So far, no taxpayer bailout has been required to save commercial banks, as has been necessary for thrift institutions (though Congress has loaned funds to the FDIC), but the extent of the bank industry's weakness is still largely unknown. Of course, it was the same way in the early stages of the S&L crisis, when banking executives and federal regulators assured congressional committees that they wouldn't have to tap the taxpayer to pay off depositors.

The Hazardous Waste Problem

Fallen banks are not the government's only expensive liability. A generation of mismanagement and abuse by Washington itself has levied huge claims on our fiscal future. Federal agencies for decades have indiscriminately dumped incredible amounts of hazardous waste at thousands of places across the country. And even after the government in the late 1970s and early 1980s fashioned laws for safely storing toxic materials and cleaning waste sites, officials at many government facilities, including nuclear plants, military bases, Agriculture Department storage sites and NASA installations, simply ignored state and federal regulations, continuing to dump hazardous and radioactive wastes wherever it was convenient.

Undoubtedly the worst case is that of the Department of Energy (DOE). Over a period of 40 years, DOE dumped millions of cubic yards of hazardous and radioactive waste in 3,300 locations scattered at 19 sites across the country. This dumping was allowed because the bombmakers emphasized production instead of safety in America's rush to retain nuclear superiority over the Russians in the early days of the atomic age and throughout the Cold War. As a result, the backyards of nuclear facilities wound up as the recipients of sludge pits and steel drums decades before the environmental consequences of such actions were considered.

For the past 15 years or so, entreaties to stop the dumping have gone unheeded. Private environmental organizations, internal Energy Department warnings and investigations by the General Accounting Office and the Environmental Protection Agency, all proved unsuccessful at deterring the indiscriminate dumping.

Although the Energy Department in the late 1980s began to recognize the enormity of its environmental errors, it was not until 1989 and the appointment of Admiral James D. Watkins as Energy secretary, that the world's largest producer of nuclear weapons truly began to consider cleaning up its past. Even now, several years after the agency began examining its toxic refuse, the full extent of the waste, along with the cost and methods for cleaning it up, are still unknown. The Energy Department first estimated that some $70 billion would be required to eliminate the hazards but, not unlike escalations of the S&L crisis, more recent, realistic assessments by the General Accounting Office figure the task will siphon off between $150 billion and $200 billion from the budget in the next 30 years. So enormous is the task that the Energy Department's budget for cleaning up hazardous and radioactive waste will soon surpass the Environmental Protection Agency's budget, which, of course, is used to monitor and clean up hazards throughout the country.

The Cleanup in the Department of Defense

The Department of Defense is now grappling with virtually the same problems that confront the Energy Department. It is perhaps a small comfort to the Pentagon that it won't be burdened with DOE's exotic, radioactive wastes for which cleanup technologies have still to be developed. Nevertheless, the military has a considerably larger cleanup job to contemplate: Approximately 17,000 hazardous waste sites have been cataloged at 1,800 defense bases and installations across the country. Some Pentagon officials estimate that the cleanup will take about 10 years and cost around $20 billion. But the Defense Department's inspector general figures on a $100 billion cleanup requiring 20 to 30 years.

The domestic budget will undoubtedly bear the brunt of these and other federal mistakes. And the impact of such enormous neglect and mismanagement on the future is obvious: that is, less money for future investments; for health care and education; for housing; and for the vast demands of the nation's social agenda.

OFF THE BOOKS

All told, the S&Ls, the commercial banks, and the government's hazardous waste disasters could end up costing taxpayers $800 billion or more in the coming decades. What is worse, however, is that this estimate does not include other, potentially more serious, risks to the government's financial stability and to the further erosion of domestic discretionary funds.

One of the biggest problems is credit exposure. Through direct loans, loan guarantees, and government-sponsored enterprises, Washington extends credit and insurance to students, farmers, savers, homeowners, and builders. But when Americans default on the government's credit, often it is their fellow citizens who get stuck with the bill.

Federal Credit and Insurance

The federal government is the country's largest source of credit, and its activities represent a significantly underestimated liability to the nation. The good news is that most of the government's credit and insurance commitments are contingent liabilities; Washington dips into the Treasury only when someone defaults or becomes insolvent. The bad news is that both the amount of federal credit extended and the rate of defaults have risen at unprecedented rates in recent years.

For instance, between 1970 and 1990, the government's total federal credit and insurance programs grew by 594 percent and loans by government-sponsored enterprises racked up an increase of nearly 3,500 percent.[35] In 1990, loan defaults and write-offs totaled $14.8 billion and losses from insurance were $92.7 billion. By comparison, in 1982, just seven years earlier, loan defaults were only $3.7 billion and insurance losses totaled just $4.6 billion.[36] At the end of 1989, the amount of federally assisted credit and insurance outstanding was a staggering $6.2 trillion.[37]

Until recently, few government officials paid much attention to this little known aspect of federal finance. But the billions lost in the S&L scandal have made federal officials more sensitive to the government's promises, its credit practices, and to the potential for huge losses in other financial areas. Of most concern have been the government-sponsored enterprises, whose outstanding obligations totaled $980 billion by the end of 1990, up from just $38.9 billion in 1970.[38]

Indeed, government credit, and thus the potential for loss, seems to be everywhere:

- Some 41 percent of all home mortgages have been guaranteed by federal agencies or securitized by government-sponsored enterprises. An additional 47 percent of home mortgages are held by banks and thrifts with deposit insurance. Thus, 88 percent of all mortgages have explicit or implicit federal backing.

- An estimated 73 percent of all farm debt has federal support, including $20 billion from the Farmers Home Administration, and another 26 percent is financed by the Farm Credit System.
- Nearly all student loans are federally guaranteed, and Sallie Mae, a government-sponsored enterprise, has financed 43 percent of them.

Future Losses in the Credit Programs

Even more troublesome than the government's existing fiscal exposure is Washington's warnings that its credit programs could suffer losses in the coming years. The Federal Housing Administration could lose 10s of billions of dollars in the next 20 years, more than half of which is the result of commitments outstanding in 1990. Slower household formation, which reduces housing appreciation, is expected to increase the number of mortgage defaults. This, in turn, could raise costs for the government's mortgage credit program. Additional losses, costing billions of dollars, are destined in the housing programs run by the Department of Veterans Affairs and the Farmers Home Administration. The housing slump and its deflated real estate prices could hasten and deepen losses for these programs.

One of the principal concerns, besides the potential for monumental losses, is the so-called moral hazard integral to government credit and insurance programs. Some government corporations have explicit guarantees from the Treasury to reimburse losses. Bank deposit insurance from the Federal Deposit Insurance Corporation is the best example. Other entities have no explicit guarantees, but government officials and financial experts have long recognized that Uncle Sam has an implicit obligation to rescue shaky and insolvent enterprises. Such was the case with the Farm Credit System, in which the implicit safety net suddenly became explicit, and a crisis required a taxpayer bailout. In 1988 the government authorized $4 billion in assistance for the failing credit system after it had lost $4.6 billion in 1985 and 1986. Earlier in the decade Fannie

Mae, the largest government-sponsored enterprise, almost went under, and in 1981 it had a negative net worth of some $11 billion. Government assistance and declining interest rates rescued the mortgage provision corporation.

The government's faith and credit have at times undermined the very system it ostensibly supports. Though the policy inherent in federal guarantees had its birth in attempts to alleviate the New Deal's banking jitters and avoid further collapse of the 1930s economy, in recent times the government's credit and insurance backing has encouraged banking institutions and government-sponsored enterprises to take imprudent business risks. Knowing that losses would be repaid by the U.S. Treasury, many banks, federally insured credit unions, and government-sponsored enterprises (GSEs) have made excessive and risky loans, entered into less than ideal business deals, and reduced the capital levels needed to sustain sound financial practices.[39] The problem often has been complicated by fraud and abuse, prevalent, for instance, in some 60 percent or more of thrift institutions taken over by federal regulators in the past several years.

The government also has compounded the problem in recent years by creating an increasing number of government-sponsored enterprises—five of which have been created since the mid-1980s. In some cases, Congress has purposely formed these *new* entities—rather than funding their activities through regular budget accounting—to make it look as though the overall federal budget deficit wasn't rising.

Though little can be done to eliminate the existing exposure of outstanding credit and insurance (the damage is already done), Congress recently has legislated changes to keep the uncharted budget from repeating such rapid unchecked growth in the future. In 1990 it distinguished between GSEs that could be excluded from federal budget totals and those that couldn't, and also changed the accounting system by which loan guarantees and other credit is expressed on the books. The new approach may also force Congress to limit credit growth since many such programs will now compete with other domestic programs for appropriations. Such fiscal discipline is long overdue.

Chapter Two

Reagan's Republic

BACK TO THE FUTURE

In the 1984 movie *Back to the Future*, actor Michael J. Fox plays Marty McFly, a teenager accidently transported back to the 1950s, where he becomes involved in the high school antics and courtship drama of his parents. In order to return to his own time, Marty hunts down the younger version of Doc Brown, played by Christopher Lloyd, the zany inventor whose time warp experiments in a Delorean automobile had transported the teenager into the past.

Doc at first refuses to believe that Marty has come from the future and tests the boy about the 1980s. He asks Marty who the president of the United States will be, but the boy's reply is unconvincing. The answer, of course, is Ronald Reagan, to which Doc incredulously responds, "The actor?" He sarcastically supposes that Jack Benny will be secretary of the treasury, and slams the door in Marty's face.

A Picture of Reagan as President

It takes considerable imagination to contemplate the Oval Office in the hands of a radio announcer turned grade-B actor, but in-between the 1950s and the 1980s, Ronald Reagan became something altogether different. The star of *Bedtime for Bonzo* and *Knute Rockne, All American* who had voted for Franklin Roosevelt and Harry Truman, donned conservative convictions and attracted well-heeled political backers. Reagan became governor of California, the country's most populous state, quelled 1960s-era student riots, and found himself in the vanguard of a growing right wing political movement. He campaigned for, and lost, the Republican presidential nomination to Gerald R. Ford in 1976. In 1980, however, Reagan won the nomination and then the presidency, the beneficiary of an electorate tired of Jimmy Carter's failed leadership.

Reagan swept the nation. He won 46 of the 50 states in the electoral college, and swiftly transformed his stunning victory into a political mandate made all the easier by the president's unusually long coattails. In 1980, Republicans took back the U.S. Senate, the first time in 26 years that the GOP had wrested control of the chamber from the Democrats. Though Republicans would hold onto the Senate for only six years, it was enough time to implement historic legislation, a combination of tax cuts, and spending shifts that would influence federal budgets for more than a decade.

Back to the Future's Doc Brown might have thought the idea of Ronald Reagan in the White House a bit less preposterous had the Delorean-turned-time machine been able to tour him through the changes the country experienced between the 1950s and the 1980s, such as the rapid growth of government entitlement programs, a hefty rise in taxes squeezing the middle class, and the increasing distrust, born of Watergate and Vietnam, with which Americans viewed their government.

Moreover, the country's relative economic and geopolitical decline that had began in the late 1960s and early 1970s continued to fuel the fears of national isolation and eclipse. The problems only worsened as the 1980s approached.

The 1970s—The Carter Presidency

Jimmy Carter's lackluster presidency didn't help. Inexperienced in the ways of Washington policy and politics, faced with an Arab oil embargo, hostages in Iran, and growing inflation, the Georgia governor and peanut farmer had trouble turning his own brand of naïve populism into effective public policy. Even relations with the Democratic Congress were dismal, at least until the Carter White House learned to play by Washington's rules. By that time, though, it was too late; in fact, many Carter initiatives never made it out of Congress. During the 1980 presidential campaign, in a debate with the incumbent president, Ronald Reagan rhetorically asked the

American people if they were better off than they had been four years earlier. In the November election, Americans answered with their votes: absolutely not.

A result of their collective decision was the most conservative American presidency in more than 50 years. Carter certainly was no liberal Democrat, at least not when it came to military spending and federal deregulation, but with Reagan the nation elected a vision of government and country that was considerably different from what actually existed at the time.

Smaller government, lower taxes, unfettered business, a powerful military supporting an unchallenged America—this was the vision Reagan offered. This was the vision of the past, of vigor and greatness, of Marty McFly and Doc Brown's 1950s. Reagan offered us a time before Toyota and Sony became household words, a time before the country's doubts crept in. And for better or worse, we accepted the offer.

THE TAX TIDE

After 16 years of complaining to anyone who would listen, a retired home appliance manufacturer named Howard Jarvis collected 1.5 million petition signatures in California to cut the state's property taxes. Long considered a nuisance, or a nut, for his tireless attacks on high taxes and bureaucratic waste, Jarvis proved to be prophetic. Millions of Californians, fed up with higher tax bills, listened to his words. In 1978 his tax-cutting Proposition 13 was approved by a 2-to-1 margin. By their votes, Californians transformed the red-faced man with the clenched fist and sagging jowls into a national symbol of middle-class resentment toward profligate government. "The only way to cut the cost of government is not to give them money in the first place," Jarvis thundered.[1]

The Tax Revolt

And so the tax revolt was born. Jarvis became a folk hero, wound up on the cover of *Time* magazine, and traveled more than 150,000 miles preaching the gospel of fiscal limits and lightened middle-class burdens. Proposition 13 chopped California taxes by more than $7 billion, a 57 percent cut, the single largest reduction in inflation-bloated property taxes since the Great Depression. Proposition 13's success and the words of Jarvis were seductive, quickly spreading throughout the country as other states adopted similar initiatives. Voters in Tennessee and Michigan approved limits on the taxing power of their states. Taxpayers in Ohio turned down 86 of 139 school tax levies, including emergency funding for schools in Cleveland and Columbus that were teetering on the brink of bankruptcy.[2]

A variety of schemes showed up on state ballots that year, even plans that presaged the 1985 Balanced Budget and Emergency Deficit Reduction Act, more commonly known as the Gramm-Rudman-Hollings Act. Many of the proposals required cuts across entire budgets, regardless of an individual program's merits. Of 16 states with tax cut propositions on the ballot in 1978, voters approved 80 percent of them.[3] It was suddenly the year of taxes: politicians both local and national, the tax and spend culprits themselves, tripped over each other in their support for trimming government budgets. At the federal level, Jimmy Carter and the Congress cut taxes by nearly $19 billion in 1978, yet overall, taxes actually increased as a result of inflation and the massive bite that came from rising Social Security payroll taxes.[4]

In October of 1978, the Senate also approved an amendment to the fiscal 1979 budget resolution that would combine limitations on government spending with a 30 percent reduction in federal income tax rates, proposed earlier by Rep. Jack Kemp (R, N.Y.) and Sen. William Roth (R, Del.). House Democrats were ready to support the deal, but it was blocked in a congressional conference committee when Carter threatened to veto the measure. The defeat would be temporary.

The shift from Howard Jarvis in 1978 to Ronald Reagan in 1980 seemed natural to many voters. In many ways the antitax revolt was simply the most potent part of an antigovernment revolt. Americans' faith in the government to solve complex problems, and its view of the government as a positive force in society, had eroded as societal problems grew alongside government's share of their paychecks. Since the Kennedy years, people had been giving government at all levels more money, for which they had not necessarily seen corresponding improvements in living conditions for themselves or for others. In 1960 total spending by government at the national, state, and local levels was $837 per person; by fiscal year 1987 it had climbed to $4,810, a vast increase even in real terms.[5]

Disenchantment with the Government

Over time, the disenchantment of the governed coalesced into contempt for the government. Polls taken by the University of Michigan portray a troubling increase in antigovernment feeling since the mid-1960s. Indeed, beginning in 1964 (not so coincidently, the year the Gulf of Tonkin incident expanded the Vietnam War), the percentage of Americans who said the federal government could be trusted "to do the right thing" started plummeting. It fell from 76 percent in 1964 to 54 percent in 1970, and then fell further to 33 percent in 1976 and down to 25 percent in 1980. In tandem, the percentage of Americans who believed that the federal government wasted tax dollars increased from under 50 percent in 1964 to more than 75 percent in 1980.[6]

CUTTING TAXES

Reagan's ascendency was not a cause of these developments, but a consequence. His promises to slash taxes and cut federal programs were made for a middle class tired of inflation and unchecked government spending.

Reagan had figured out the populist value of tax cuts on his own, even before the Jarvis juggernaut. As governor of California, Reagan had promoted a 1973 amendment (ultimately defeated) to limit the taxing authority of the state. Reagan's heart, though, was in spending cuts. Like most traditional conservatives, in his campaigns for the Oval Office, Reagan initially insisted that federal expenditures be reduced before taxes were cut in order to avoid crippling deficits.

Reagan should have stuck to his guns. Some conservative politicians and economists, namely Jack Kemp, economist Arthur Laffer, and a former *Wall Street Journal* editorial writer

named Jude Wanniski, convinced Reagan in the months leading up to the 1980 election that supply-side economics could
solve the country's fiscal woes. Garden variety conservatives
had long embraced tax cuts as part of their program to curb
government growth, but the new strain of supply-siders encouraged the reductions as a way to actually *increase* federal
revenues. They reasoned that tax cuts would stimulate private
sector investment, which in turn would stabilize the economy,
raise the national income level, and produce additional tax dollars. The money would supplement domestic program cuts
used to finance higher defense spending—all without increasing the size of the government.

Supply-Side Policies

Not everyone on Reagan's campaign team bought the supply-
side arguments. Some of his economic advisers suspected that
more money in the hands of the public, even the prospect of it,
would only worsen inflation. And a cut in taxes when government spending still was climbing would simply serve to widen
the deficit, critics said. Nonetheless, the faddish fiscal ideas
proved irresistible to Reagan, a politician asking Americans to
embrace an improbable economic program: that taxes could be
cut, spending slashed, government tamed, inflation flattened,
business regulations dismantled, interest rates lowered, defense strengthened, and the budget balanced.

Of course, for Reagan strategists, it didn't hurt that by latch-
ing onto supply-side policies they virtually eliminated any
presidential challenge from Jack Kemp or others from the far
right of the Republican or Conservative parties.

Americans by and large knew that cuts in federal spending
would require national sacrifice. In 1980, a majority of them
still supported the reductions, though their enthusiasm would
wane as the decade progressed. Waste and abuse could surely
be cut, they thought, and the programs for the poor that had so
greatly expanded during the 1970s, could be trimmed. And although many Americans frowned on big government, their
votes for Ronald Reagan did not, for the most part, translate
into a mandate for dismantling the welfare state. Even Jack

Kemp had warned that neither the country nor the Congress would sit idly by if Reagan took his axe to such mainstays as Social Security. Opinion polls on the eve of Reagan's Republic indicated that taxpayers favored cuts in programs for the poor more than in other areas, but that a majority could not be found to support cuts in any specific program. Ambivalence, contradiction, and disagreement were the hallmarks of the nation's debate on federal spending. Indeed, the same survey in which almost three-quarters of the country approved of Reagan's spending cuts also demonstrated that nearly two-thirds agreed that the government has an obligation to help the poor.[7]

A decade later, nothing much had changed. A 1989 poll by CBS News found that 65 percent of Americans believed the federal government has a responsibility to help people pay for a college education if they can't afford it; 71 percent said the government should help people pay for nursing homes or for other long-term medical care; and 57 percent thought it the government's responsibility to provide health insurance coverage for those people that don't have it.[8] This was, and still is, a country where the public sees little contradiction between low taxes and expansive entitlement programs.

Of course, there had been tax cuts before Reagan was elected president. Though tax reductions today are commonly associated with Republicans as a result of that party's clever politicking—as well as the perennial failure of Democrats to beat the rap on taxing and spending—one of the largest cuts in history came from the Kennedy administration. Proposed at the end of 1962 but not enacted until early 1964, shortly after Kennedy's death, the tax cut reduced individual income tax rates across the spectrum. It was estimated at the time that the Treasury's annual revenue loss would be about $14 billion, some 2 percent of that period's GNP.[9]

A historic irony took root in the Kennedy tax cut. Proposed and enacted by Democrats to jump start the economy by increasing government spending relative to revenues, they counted on the cuts to raise total spending by increasing the public's demand for goods, which over time would boost output and employment. Though the Democrats also claimed what later would be called supply-side benefits from the cuts (especially for the richest Americans), encouraging additional private investment was not as important to them as was an economy at full employment.

Almost two decades later, the conservative supply-siders would embrace the Kennedy tax cut as their own. Trumpeting the modest revenue increases that resulted from the 1964 tax reductions as proof that their theory was sound, the conservatives proposed a 30 percent tax rate reduction to prime the economic pump and increase government revenues that the cuts themselves would eliminate.

Demand-Siders versus Supply-Siders

One of the important differences between Kennedy's demand-siders and Reagan's supply-siders, though, was that the increase in total output would be immediate and sizable in the conservative scenario. And for that crucial element in Reagan's fiscal proposal, there was no precedent. The Kennedy tax cut experience on which the supply-siders were relying to justify their claims had actually produced rather mixed results. Total output, spending, and employment all increased and unemployment fell after the 1964 tax cut. But as Herbert Stein, a conservative economist and chairman of Richard Nixon's Council of Economic Advisers, notes, the increases of output and employment have never been plausibly explained as a victory for supply-siders, nor was the increase in revenues. Rather, growth in the demand side that had begun before the reductions were implemented, combined with a small amount of inflation, were the more likely causes.[10] On the eve of Reagan's historic tax cuts, Walter Heller, chairman of Kennedy and Johnson's Council of Economic Advisers, raised inflation's spectre, another reason why the Kennedy tax cut so frequently cited by the supply-siders simply didn't apply. "Savings stimulated by the 1964 tax cut came from real marginal rate cuts in a non-inflationary environment, not illusory ones that high inflation in the Eighties will snatch away."[11]

The lesson of history was conveniently ignored. The Reagan administration's first tax proposal was virtually identical to the initial Kemp-Roth legislation from the late 1970s. Reagan wanted to cut individual tax rates by 30 percent (10 percent each year for three years) and provide tax relief for business, mainly through more liberal depreciation allowances and research and development tax credits. Under the plan introduced to Congress February 18, 1981, in a prime-time television address, the marginal tax rates would be compressed. The 70 percent rate would be reduced to 50 percent, and the 14 percent rate would be cut to 10 percent.

Economists held their breath and concerned politicians drew up battle plans. Indeed, on the day Reagan introduced the tax cut, Harvard economist Otto Eckstein warned that much of the supply-side program had never been tested. Eckstein urged a go-slow approach, cautioning that anything else "would be a gamble with our economic system."[12]

A debate in Congress began in earnest during April, just days after Reagan was shot by John Hinckley, Jr., outside the Washington Hilton on March 30. On April 10, the Senate Budget Committee rejected the Reagan administration's budget plan, fearing a skyrocketing budget deficit. Some thought that the Kemp-Roth formula was finally dead. But they underestimated Reagan's ability to rally the Republican faithful. After a stern presidential speech in late April, the budget resolution was passed. And it included the framework of the president's controversial tax proposal.

The Tax Cut Victory

There were other rough moments for the Reagan plan, the largest tax cut in the nation's history, but after April there was little doubt that the Economic Recovery Tax Act of 1981 (ERTA), as the legislation was formally known, would be approved. There were compromises: A short delay implementing the cuts and a reduction in the first-year cut from 10 percent to 5 percent. Still, the joy of victory was Reagan's when the bill cleared Congress in early August.

Democrats still smarting from the loss of the Senate the previous year went along with the legislation to avoid the possibility of a further electoral rout. Many legislators who figured on negative consequences of the cuts attempted to pin the blame on the White House: "Make no mistake about it. This is the President's bill," Rep. Dan Rostenkowski (D, Ill.), chairman of the House Ways and Means Committee and a powerful player in national tax policy, reportedly stressed to colleagues before the final vote. "It outlines a bold—and risky—economic strategy. Only time will tell whether the risks involved . . . were worth taking."[13] Political backpeddling aside, lopsided victories of 67 to 8 in the Senate and 282 to 95 in the House meant that scores of Democrats, try as they would in later years, could never truly disassociate themselves from the cut's consequences. Indeed, they are as much to blame as the Republicans and the Reagan administration for the decade's historic deficits and the government's disinvestment in domestic agencies.

The 1981 Recession

The 1981 tax cut became to supporters and critics alike a symbol of the Reagan administration's economic policies. One of the most painful recessions of the 20th century came crashing down on the nation at about the same time as the tax cuts. The downturn mainly was the untimely result of the Federal Reserve Board's struggle to end a decade of ravaging inflation, but the 1981–82 economic bust was seen by Democrats and even some conservatives as evidence that the supply-side wisdom was anything but wise.

Democrats soon began shouting in the wind, accusing Reagan of gambling with the country's prosperity and the prospect of higher federal deficits for the sake of lower taxes. Conservatives defended the supply-side banner, and instead blamed the sudden recession on the inability of Congress to enact everything that Reagan had requested. Arthur Laffer, one of the supply-siders who had helped to convince Reagan of the program, even pinned the recession on the short postponement of the tax cut that Reagan agreed to in order to ease ERTA's passage among legislators who worried about its impact on the deficit.[14]

THE DEFENSE DYNAMO

In the final months of Ronald Reagan's second term, a president on his way out met with Mikhail Gorbachev, a president on his way up, to discuss the future of their troops and weapons facing off across the borders of Europe. The two leaders were to put the finishing touches on an arms reduction agreement that would give the Soviet chief what he needed most: Time and cash—in the form of presumably lower defense expenditures—to help ease explosive economic pressures at home.

Though the meetings were successful, Gorbachev had become irritated with Reagan's unwillingness to embrace even deeper reductions. Reagan had been characteristically wary, insisting that the United States could trust the Soviet Union's motives and actions, but that it would also seek to verify that the Russians were upholding their end of the bargains. Indeed, Reagan had used the phrase "trust but verify" so many times during his meetings with Gorbachev that, at one point, the Soviet leader turned to Reagan and remarked that the American president seemed to say little else.

Gorbachev may have been correct about Reagan's one-track warning, but he perhaps little appreciated the extent to which the American president had progressed philosophically. It had been a long road for Reagan, a conservative to the core, but one who seemed to genuinely dream of a safer world. Reagan's dalliance with a nuclear-free Europe at his Reykjavik meeting with Gorbachev showed that inside this cold warrior was a warmth and hope rarely revealed. The president's followers back home were horrified about what almost happened at Reykjavik, about the thaw in relations with the Soviet Union, and even about the pending treaty. Years of caution and saber-rattling against what Reagan called the *evil empire* seemed to vanish in the mist from which it was created; the man who had sought to return the multipolar world of the 1980s to the bipolar rhetoric of the 1950s appeared, to those on the right, toward the end of his term to abandon his visceral anti-Communism.

Conservatives would later assert that the remarkable events at decade's end, the crumbling of Communism, the spread of democracy, and nascent market economies through much of Eastern Europe, were the result of Reagan's policies: The weapons buildup designed to keep America strong militarily and the economic and military aid offered to those foreign regimes, both legitimate governments and rebels, that promised to further democratic aims.

Scholars will no doubt for years debate whether the Iron Curtain ultimately rusted from decades of economic and political erosion, from being buffeted by the winds of military competition, Western cultural materialism, or from some combination of forces. What is clear, however, is that by the twilight of his presidency, Ronald Reagan faced an evil empire that could no longer afford to be either. When Reagan faced Gorbachev for the last time as president, the two leaders met in New York harbor under the gaze of the Statue of Liberty. Of the two men, only Reagan led a nation that remained a global superpower. The victory was not without costs, however, as the budgets of many domestic agencies, grown stagnant to power the defense buildup, receded along with Soviet forces.

DRAMATIC DIFFERENCE

Matters had appeared much differently eight years previously. In many ways the 1970s had not been kind to America or its perception of itself. Vietnam's legacy still haunted the public and its leaders; the armed forces remained unpopular on college campuses and underfunded, at least by recent standards, in Congress. Defense spending in 1975 hit its lowest point in decades, having dropped 33 percent in real terms between 1968 and 1975.[17] By the time Jimmy Carter was elected president (ironically in part by campaigning to cut defense spending), neglect of the Pentagon was beginning to take its toll. Army Chief of Staff General Edward C. Meyer warned of a "hollow army," an armed force whose readiness and preparedness had significantly deteriorated. To keep down costs during the Vietnam War, the Pentagon had depleted much of its worldwide stock of ammunition and had since avoided a much-needed restructuring and modernization of the armed forces. The result was a poorly prepared and equipped fighting force with limited public or political support, and with little sense of mission.

As the country's respect for its military dwindled, so did its sense of global power, and its ability to dominate events internationally. A set of failed military exploits further ruined the nation's image of itself as any kind of a superpower. Gerald R. Ford's botched 1975 rescue of hostages aboard the cargo ship *Mayaguez* off the Cambodian coast was compounded in the spring of 1980 by the fiery end in a Mideast desert of Carter's ill-fated rescue of Iranian-held embassy hostages. Indeed, it was the country itself, its military, its sense of dignity and future, that during the crisis seemed to be hostages.

The Role of Military Spending in the United States and the Soviet Union

Military experts point out that the United States picked a poor time to neglect its armed forces and brood over its seemingly diminished capacity to influence international events. At the same time America was trimming its military budget, the Soviet Union had accelerated its own weapons modernization program. By 1976, the Soviet Union's military spending was some 41 percent higher than that of the United States, and it continued to pour funds into guns instead of butter throughout the late 1970s.[18]

Just as the spending gap between the cold warriors seemed greatest, the Soviets invaded Afghanistan and Iranian revolutionaries took over the American embassy in Tehran. Although Carter had not cut the defense budget as promised, Pentagon spending essentially remained stable at less than 5 percent of the gross national product and 23 percent of federal outlays for the first two years of his administration.[19] Under pressure from a public and Congress belatedly concerned with the country's deteriorating military capacity, Carter in the final two years of his term added funds to his defense budget. Though many Americans associate the vast increase in military spending solely with Reagan, it was Carter who began reversing a decade-long slide in the Pentagon's budget. Starting in 1979,

Carter supported 5 percent increases in real defense spending as part of a deal struck with the Senate to ratify the Strategic Arms Limitation Talks. And though the treaty was never approved, a casualty of a more conservative U.S. defense policy and the Soviet invasion of Afghanistan, the Pentagon budget hikes remained.

There is no disputing Ronald Reagan's stand on defense: only more of it would do. In his 1980 campaign for the White House, Reagan initially proposed a 5 percent real increase in defense spending, but raised it to 7 percent after Carter's 1980 budget included a 5 percent rise. Though Carter had pushed the defense budget up by more than 10 percent in real terms in the final years of his presidency, Americans were so exasperated with the president that Reagan succeeded in portraying the Georgian as soft on defense.

That Carter would have continued the defense buildup at anywhere near the level Reagan engineered in the early 1980s is unlikely. Toward the end of 1980, in fact, some of Carter's advisers felt that the budget increases had already done much to fill the gaps left by earlier underfunding, and that the administration could turn its attention to more pressing matters.

The mythic Ronald Reagan, the cold warrior, the visceral anti-Communist, spent virtually his entire presidency espousing and assembling a mightier military and a bigger defense budget to support it. In Caspar Weinberger, his secretary of defense, Reagan found an ally who would entertain little but ever-expanding budget authority for the military. To old Washington hands, Weinberger's inflexibility was a bit curious, since the defense secretary had earlier in his career earned the name "Cap the Knife" for his ruthless cost-cutting while director of Nixon's White House budget office.

Reagan knew the mood of the nation when he pursued, and won, the presidency by promising to help America stand tall again in the eyes of the world. He aimed to keep his promise by spending $2.2 trillion on defense during his presidency, creating the largest peacetime buildup of military personnel and equipment in the nation's history. Reagan in his first term of office pushed a 53 percent real increase in defense spending through a divided Congress. Averaging some 12 percent a year, the rate of spending in the early 1980s was higher than it was during Vietnam. Writes Lawrence J. Korb, assistant secretary of defense for personnel at that time: "It is no exaggeration to say that in the Reagan years the Defense Department enjoyed a wartime buildup without a war."[20] It was this historic rise in military spending, combined with the revenue shortfalls created by Reagan's tax cuts, that exacerbated not only the federal deficit but—through austerity in nondefense budgets—hollow government.

National defense rose steadily, from 23.2 percent of the federal budget and 5.3 percent of GNP in 1981 to a peak of 28.1 percent of the budget in 1987 and 6.5 percent of the gross national product in 1986.[21] Prior to 1986, defense spending had last surpassed 6.5 percent of GNP in 1972, as the Vietnam War was winding to a close.

The Pentagon's buildup was made to last, for the greatest growth in defense spending came in multiyear procurement, not in troops. The Pentagon's budget authority for bombers, submarines, and other large weapons systems grew a formidable 115 percent in real terms between 1980 and 1985. Conversely, budget authority for military personnel grew by just 3 percent in real terms during the same period.[22]

Mismanagement of Pentagon Defense Spending

As much as the vast increase in defense procurement budgets helped the economies of California, Massachusetts, and other defense industry-intense states, it created significant management problems for the Department of Defense. Indeed, some critics charged that the nation received more mismanagement than new weapons for its defense dollars in the 1980s. The Pentagon simply did not have in place enough qualified procurement specialists and contract managers to handle the rapidly filling pipeline of sophisticated weapons and the private companies that profited from consulting, designing, building, and testing the country's planes, tanks, missiles, and submarines.

Perceptions of widespread Pentagon waste, fraud, and abuse sharpened as news stories began to detail the purchase of

$5,000 hammers, $7,000 coffee machines, and $600 toilet seats. This perception was reinforced in 1985, when the Congressional Budget Office suggested that an increase in the nation's military capabilities had not accompanied the greater Pentagon spending. The number of weapons purchased, for instance, increased more slowly than did real acquisition budgets.

In short, the Pentagon was spending more and getting less for its money, as inflation, technological advances, and mismanaged contracts combined to make military hardware ever more expensive. Jacques S. Gansler, a military analyst and member of the 1986 Blue Ribbon Commission on Defense Management, estimates that real (inflation-adjusted) unit costs tend to rise 5 percent and 7 percent annually for every new generation of equipment.[23]

Examples are evident throughout the Pentagon's catalog of sophisticated weapons: The Air Force in 1951 paid $7 billion (in 1983 dollars) for 6,300 airplanes. By 1983, $11 billion bought the service only 322 fighters.[24] Four billion additional dollars actually bought nearly 6,000 fewer aircraft. Moreover, Reagan purchased 6 percent more missiles than Carter did, but it cost him 91 percent more in constant dollars. Reagan ordered 30 percent more tanks, but it cost him almost three times as much as similar hardware cost Carter.[25]

The High Cost of Weapons

The more sophisticated the weapons, the longer their production seemed to take and the higher seemed to be the cost overruns. The surprisingly unassailable performance of American weaponry during Desert Storm notwithstanding, Pentagon procurement winds up being for Congress's folks back home instead of soldiers in the field. It's not just that the Defense Department and its contractors weren't good at estimating schedules for military hardware, but the high cost of weapons systems also became part of the problem. The huge expense entailed in making modern killing machines encourages both the Pentagon and prospective manufacturers to underestimate the costs of weapons in order to get Congress to approve the necessary funds. Estimates of the projects suddenly rise only after millions, if not billions, have been spent, which leaves legislators with the unhappy choice of either killing the project—wasting billions, putting thousands of people out of work, and possibly crippling national defense—or spending untold billions more to see planes, submarines, or missiles to completion. In fact, costs including inflation for military weapons systems on average double between the initial appropriations estimate given to Congress by the Pentagon and the final cost of the hardware.[26]

Indeed, almost all of our modern arsenal ends up over budget. The B-1 bomber. The B-2 bomber. The Trident submarine. The Strategic Defense Initiative, better known as Star Wars. The Navy's A-12 attack plane, whose development expense in 1990 was so out of line that it ultimately cost the program managers and an undersecretary of defense their jobs. Finally, the plane itself was sacked when contractors could not give Defense Secretary Richard Cheney reliable information about the fighter's production costs.

Estimates for the B-2 Stealth bomber, designed as a replacement to B-52s and supposedly capable of penetrating Soviet air space, have steadily increased. Congress was so outraged by the B-2's massive cost (about $880 million per copy) that it has supplied the Pentagon funds for only one half of the 150 planes it originally wanted. By 1991, the $31 billion spent on the B-2 had bought 15 of the aircraft. The White House has fought for another 60 copies while B-2 opponents have continued to criticize the plane. Rep. Les Aspin (D, WI.), chairman of the House Armed Services Committee, and others sought to eliminate, or at least further reduce, funding for the bomber, which they view as an expensive relic of the Cold War. Finally, new production was shut down in 1991.

The Elimination or Reduction of Weapons

Moreover, stretching out programs became a favorite Reagan tactic. By pushing more and more weapons into the development pipeline and then slowing their production rate to accommodate declining budgets, the Reagan administration sought to power their defense buildup even after they had departed the White House. That strategy has worked to some extent: Even though congressional pressure successfully cut the defense budget and slowed the buildup beginning in 1986 (the year the Democrats again controlled the Senate), pressure on procurement budgets continued to grow as a result of past decisions to build expensive new weapons systems. So many new weapons systems were begun during the 1980s that even the sizable defense budget Reagan left for Bush was not large enough to pay for all the programs he had initiated. As the defense buildup slowed, declining by 11 percent in real terms between 1986 and 1989, Reagan's budgeteers simply stretched out procurement schedules rather than making rational cuts to any part of the budget.

Thus, Bush inherited an estimated $400 billion defense program, but only a $300 billion defense budget. Lawrence Korb has figured that more than $1 trillion worth of hardware clogged the defense pipeline by the end of the 1980s. Paying for all of it is more unlikely than ever, considering that the Pentagon's spending in the Cold War's thaw is now fast declining. Personnel levels alone are supposed to be cut 25 percent by mid-1995.

Just how the Pentagon and Congress plan to achieve these reductions remains to be seen. Congress has made little attempt to cut expensive weapons systems even though the Pentagon in 1990 and 1991 told legislators that it was willing to cut several programs to meet reduced budget targets, including production of a new Marine Corps helicopter and such outdated airplanes as the T-46. But Congress, more concerned with keeping jobs in their districts than reducing the deficit, refused to eliminate them. Indeed, Defense Secretary Cheney has attempted to eliminate the V-22 Osprey Marine helicopter since 1989 on the grounds that it is too expensive. But congressional delegations from Texas and Pennsylvania, where the helicopter would be built, have managed to keep the program going.

Similarly, the House Armed Services Committee has voted nearly $1 billion to keep production lines open to rebuild such older aircraft as the F-14, made by Long Island-based Grumman Corp., which otherwise would have virtually no defense manufacturing work.

As a result, the Pentagon not only ends up with equipment it contends is unnecessary, but which will cost considerably more, and in some cases, be delivered years later than first anticipated. Meanwhile, domestic agencies and social programs remain underfunded as demands for government services continue to rise.

REGULATORY REDUX

In contrast to his "only more would do" approach to defense spending, Ronald Reagan's attitude toward regulation was "only less would do."

Looking back, Reagan was surprisingly successful. What the president sought was nothing less than a rollback of the regulation and red tape that government imposed on business and society. To those who led the charge, it was of little consequence that the regulatory assault sometimes defied, and typically ignored, laws established, in some cases, more than a century ago.

Regulation of commerce had begun in the late 19th century, a product of Washington's effort to curb monopolies and promote competition, to protect the public against "snake oil" salesmen and the purveyors of patent medicines. The Interstate Commerce Commission was created in 1887. Congress passed the Sherman Antitrust Act in 1889. The predecessor of today's Food and Drug Administration came into being on New Year's Day, 1907. And the Federal Trade Commission was established by the 1914 Clayton Act.

Franklin Roosevelt's response to the Great Depression of the 1930s was a New Deal—and a lot more regulation. Roosevelt created the Securities and Exchange Commission to stabilize financial markets. The National Labor Relations Board was given the power to remedy unfair labor practices and protect workers' rights to organize. The Federal Communications Commission regulated radio, television, and telephones to serve the public's interest. And the Civil Aeronautics Board (now the Federal Aviation Administration) told airlines where they could fly, and under what conditions.

A nation increasingly concerned with its quality of life in the 1960s and 1970s sought Washington's help to further regulate business. In 1973, the Occupational Safety and Health Administration was created to protect workers' safety and health on the job. Injury and death from mass-produced merchandise were guarded against by the Consumer Product Safety Commission. Widespread pollution problems brought into existence the Environmental Protection Agency.

Thus, the nation entered the 1980s weighed down by a century of regulation. By the time Ronald Reagan took office, the federal government was promulgating thousands of new rules every year. Not surprisingly, manufacturers and other business interests contended that the compliance burden was excessive and increasingly anticompetitive. American industry, for example, was obliged to install smokestack scrubbers to curb air pollution—an obligation overseas competitors often didn't have to contend with. And American pharmaceutical firms complained of a labyrinth of drug approval procedures—and pointed out that British, German, and Swiss competitors could get their products to market much faster.

OMB, POLITICS, AND RULES

The Reagan regulatory rout was led by the Office of Management and Budget (OMB). Once merely another cog in the executive branch's bureaucratic wheel, OMB powered that wheel after Richard Nixon reorganized the budget office and elevated it to a position of federal dominance.

Even so, not until Reagan had any president succeeded in taming the disparate agencies and departments that manage federal programs. Many had tried, Nixon and Carter most notably, but it took Reagan's conservative stamp, administered by OMB, to truly make the executive branch succumb to a single president's political philosophy. Perhaps more than any president since Roosevelt, in fact, Reagan altered the power structure in the direction of the Oval Office.

Office of Information and Regulatory Affairs (OIRA)

In 1981, Reagan issued an executive order mandating cost-benefit review of all regulatory proposals by the Office of Information and Regulatory Affairs (OIRA), an OMB unit set up in 1980 by Congress with an eye to lightening the paperwork burden federal agencies imposed on business and the general public. In 1985, the president signed another executive order strengthening OMB's power to block agency regulations by requiring agencies to inform the White House of all plans for new rules to assure consistency with administration policy.

Sunshine laws that apply to the activities of many agencies don't apply to the White House and its offices, which conveniently allowed Reagan officials to manage their revolution largely hidden from the public's view—or its accountability. Suddenly the agencies, and the Congress as well, found themselves at the mercy of an often politically motivated presidential office, and unable to prevent the White House from issuing regulations they didn't like.

Many members of Congress contend that this was never its intent in creating OIRA. But so far the legislature has had little success in countering this powerful assertion of White House power, although it has tried: Congress refused to authorize OIRA operations between 1983 and 1986, forcing OIRA to get funds from OMB's general appropriations. OIRA again was without an authorization between 1989 and 1992 as part of an ongoing battle to renew the 1980 Paperwork Reduction Act. Congress put off confirmation hearings for a new OIRA administrator, which left the agency rudderless for almost the entire tenure of Bush's presidency.

Nevertheless, OIRA has managed a regulatory retreat over the last decade. Those agencies having the greatest potential impact on the activities of the nation's business increasingly found their statutory mandate for rulemaking hindered by OMB's approval process. The Occupational Safety and Health Administration (OSHA) found its authority to regulate America's workplace thwarted most. Between 1981 and 1989, the Department of Labor (primarily OSHA and the Mine Safety and

Health Administration) had 43 percent of its regulations returned, changed, or withdrawn at OIRA's direction.[27] In all,
three federal agencies or cabinet departments had more than
one-third of their regulations stymied during the 1980s, and
eight had one-quarter of their rules delayed, changed, or
rejected.[28] The Department of Housing and Urban Development, the Education Department, the Small Business Administration, the Environmental Protection Agency, and the
Department of Health and Human Services each found their
authority to issue regulations blunted.

In the last three years of the Reagan presidency, OIRA successfully changed 22 percent of all new federal regulations.[29]
Indeed, it was Bush, as Reagan's vice president for eight years,
who as chairman of the federal Task Force on Regulatory Relief,
managed the conservatives' deregulatory program.

Ironically, intervention and obstruction by OIRA was worse
in 1989, under George Bush's supposedly moderate Republican
administration, than at any time since the White House began
to impose partisan values over the professional judgments of
agency officials. During 1989, OIRA changed, returned, or
forced agencies to withdraw some 24 percent of all government
regulations. Nearly two-thirds of HUD's regulations were challenged, along with 60 percent of the Labor Department's rules,
and almost 40 percent of the regulations proposed by the Environmental Protection Agency (EPA) and the Education
Department.[30]

What's more, the time it took for OIRA to review controversial regulations, those it returned to agencies, rose from an average of 123 days in 1988 to 194 days in 1989. OMB Watch, a
private, nonpartisan organization that scrutinizes the White
House budget office, reveals that the use of delay by the agency
would be even more apparent if a new category had not been
created for reviewing regulations in 1989. When the new "sus-
pension" category is combined with other categories as it was
in previous years, OIRA took 205 days on average to review
controversial regulations—before rejecting them.

The delays, rejections, and suspensions of agency regulations have done much to weaken, postpone, and simply derail
federal authority to oversee health and safety issues through-

out the country. Whether OMB's partisan intervention leads to such 1990 changes as deleting (thus weakening) major portions of an EPA Superfund liability rule or to long delays in the late 1980s over rules regulating tampons after problems with toxic shock syndrome, the result is the same. One EPA-proposed ruling, on handling solid waste at hazardous waste facilities, took OMB nearly two years, and two administrations, from October 1988 to July 1990, to publish in the *Federal Register* for public comment, the first round of OMB review. Equally troubling in 1990 was the reemergence of a secret cabinet-level review group that, like the old Taskforce on Regulatory Relief, began undermining—in private—regulations that the White House had agreed to in public. Led by Vice President Dan Quayle, the President's Council on Competitiveness has attempted to systematically weaken health, safety, and environmental rules for the benefit of special interests.

Agencies of the federal government with statutory authority to regulate society on behalf of public health and safety are continuously hampered, and at times prevented, from fulfilling their mission. Whether pollution or consumer products, workplace safety or unsafe drugs, agencies must first fight the White House before they can fight the problems for which they exist to remedy.

ELIMINATING ENFORCEMENT

The partisan deregulatory stance of the Reagan administration throughout the 1980s did more than simply prevent federal agencies from issuing strong regulations protecting safety and health. It contributed to the undermining of the nation's laws and regulations and was in part responsible for such financial catastrophes as the savings and loan industry scandal.

Through a systematic campaign waged by OMB and the White House, regulatory agencies across Washington were co-opted by conservative Reagan loyalists whose views ran counter to the basic missions of the agencies they would administer and to their mandates derived from congressional statute. As administrators of Washington's regulatory world, these political appointees would spend most of Reagan's two terms in the Oval Office attempting to dismantle, or at the least make ineffective, nearly a century of government oversight. By de-emphasizing regulatory agendas and starving agencies of funds for staff and enforcement programs when necessary, the White House attempted nothing less than a coordinated reduction in business and social regulation across the federal government.

There was James Watt, for instance, head of the Denver-based Mountain States Legal Foundation, a western pro-development group which regularly clashed with conservationists over environmental policies. When Watt became Reagan's first secretary of the interior, this contentious, right-wing lawyer and a group of like-minded people diligently worked to undermine decades of legislation and regulations limiting development on public lands. Pollution violations were ignored, timber and mining infractions committed by private industry in national forests went unchallenged, fees for cutting, drilling, grazing, and prospecting often went uncollected.

For instance, the General Accounting Office reports that the government has verified oil and gas production on less than 3 percent of the leases from which it derives royalties, which seriously hampers its ability to obtain the money it is owed. Part of the reason is a shortage of government inspectors, which has allowed production abuses and other violations by drilling companies to go undetected.[31]

Attempts to Deregulate the Environmental Protection Agency

Reaganites pushed deregulation at the Environmental Protection Agency (EPA) also. Charged with curbing pollution of the nation's air, water, and ground, the EPA under Reagan often ignored environmental laws and all but shut down the agency's enforcement efforts. The agency's first administrator, Anne Burford, even attempted to repeal restrictions on lead in gasoline and on dumping toxic wastes into unlined landfills. Attempts to strengthen pollution laws and further develop the agency's environmental protection mandate essentially were abandoned. So egregious were the EPA's violations during the Reagan era, that several top agency administrators were forced from office; at least one, Rita Lavelle, assistant administrator for solid waste and emergency response, was found guilty in federal court of perjury.

Federal Regulation

Indeed, when it came to federal regulation in the 1980s, the only rule was that Washington was not to offend or burden business. This was to have unfortunate consequences, however. Individuals and the nation as a whole suffered from ignored safety and health regulations, but equally tragic, taxpayers ended up footing the bill in the conservatives' rush to deregulate. And what the Reagan administration was unable to accomplish by blocking new regulations and lightening up on the laws, it did by cutting back on agencies' budgets. Virtually no regulatory agency, no enforcement unit of the federal government, was left untouched. Consigned to wither away during the 1980s, for example, were the Food and Drug Administration, the Department of Justice's Antitrust Division, the EPA's enforcement units, the investigative operations at the Federal Savings and Loan Insurance Corporation and Federal Home Loan Bank Board, the Agriculture Department's meat and poultry inspection system, and the FAA's aircraft maintenance inspection program.

The starving of agencies has had consequences for public safety, for fraud and abuse, and for the overall deterioration of federal enforcement activities:

- Taxpayers will pick up the more than $130 billion (plus interest) tab to pay off insured depositors in the savings and loan industry's collapse, in part, because numerous pleas by the government's banking agencies in the mid-1980s for additional examiners to investigate the crumbling thrift system went unheeded.

- The Federal Trade Commission spent most of the decade on the sidelines. Not a single major case was brought to trial by the commission during Reagan's two terms in office, in part because there were not enough funds in the FTC's budget to prepare big cases. A host of other regulatory entities, from the Consumer Product Safety

Commission to the Federal Communications Commission, brought fewer cases to trial for similar reasons. Staff at the Antitrust Division of the Department of Justice was cut nearly in half during the 1980s, undermining the unit's ability to protect Americans from free market abuses.

- In an attempt to privatize or make voluntary the government's meat and poultry inspections, the Reagan administration cut back the budget and staff for the Agriculture Department's inspection units. Looser regulations and fewer inspectors, in part, has led to an alarming rise in dirty and diseased chickens being processed and sold to consumers, critics charge. Chickens that would have been routinely condemned and ordered destroyed a decade ago now end up on supermarket shelves.[32] In 1985 the Agriculture Department revealed that some 35 percent of chicken carcasses were contaminated with salmonella. By 1989, four years later, Agriculture Department tests of five Southeast processing plants—the country's busiest poultry-producing region—discovered salmonella levels of nearly 60 percent.[33]

- During the 1980s the number of drug and food inspections conducted by the Food and Drug Administration declined by more than 40 percent.[34] An agency swamped by new laws and a swiftly growing generic drug industry found itself, in the aftermath of staff and budget cuts, unable to effectively regulate new drugs and protect the nation's health. Laws require the FDA to review new drug applications within six months, but the time it takes the agency to comply peaked at 31 months near the end of the 1980s. It's no wonder, really. The FDA's budgeted staff for fiscal year 1991 was about 8,440, just slightly more than were at the agency in 1980. During that period, however, Congress enacted 21 new laws covering every facet of the FDA's responsibilities.

- Similarly, the Occupational Safety and Health Administration became increasingly reactive and behind schedule during Reagan's presidency. In recent years, health inspections have been driven by complaints, leaving fewer resources for targeted inspections. Some OSHA area offices in 1988 were still working on 1985 inspection cycles.[35] And in cases where OSHA enforced its regula-

tions by issuing fines, the agency rarely collected anywhere near the amount levied against violators. Indeed,
OSHA has bargained down the fines it sets by an average of 67.5 percent. In 35 of OSHA's largest cases, the
agency collected the entire fine in just three instances.

HOLLOW AGENCIES

Of course, Ronald Reagan sought not only to curb government
regulation, but simply to curb the government. Both because of
his ideology and to pay for his defense buildup, Reagan sought
steep budget cuts on government's domestic side. The implementation of his conservative politics required that the government, like some overgrown hedge, be trimmed back and
brought under control.

Indiscriminate Cutting of Programs

Reagan, unfortunately, rarely differentiated between bureaucracy that was redundant and wasteful, on the one hand, and
government services upon which citizens across the country
depended, on the other. Thus, Reagan's White House wielded
its chopping knife without distinction, eliminating staff and
crippling programs at dozens of federal agencies. Federal
programs critical to Americans everywhere were carved up
just as energetically as those that catered to just a minority
constituency or enterprises which had outlived their usefulness.

Reagan ignored the nation's dynamic growth, what America
had become, in his quest to push Washington back several
mythical decades. Even so, the expansion of the country and
its economy has far outpaced the ability of the government to
keep up. Americans' demand for services from Washington
have escalated as society has grown and become more complex. In seemingly every area touched by government (i.e., immigration, crime, drugs, pollution, commerce, transportation,
agriculture, and urban affairs), the need for Washington to do
more was as clearly evident when Reagan became president as
it is today.

Yet these needs were not met with any commensurate increase in budget. In many cases, just the opposite happened. After years of racking up gradual gains to cope with increased responsibilities, many agencies in the 1980s saw their budgets cut in the cause of deficit reduction and conservative politics.

Prices increased by nearly 50 percent between 1980 and 1989. Just to keep pace with inflation, then, an agency's budget in the 1980s would have needed to grow 50 percent over the decade; and while some agencies grew that much or more, certainly they were the exceptions.

By far, the biggest hits were borne by the General Services Administration and the Labor Department: Their budgets in 1989 were 58 percent and 28 percent, respectively, below their 1980 levels. Other agencies pinched in the decade include the Commerce Department, down 11 percent, and the Environmental Protection Agency, cut 8 percent, in the same period.[36]

Plenty of other budgets and programs were cut during the 1980s; and those lucky enough to miss OMB's knife were for the most part still not in great shape; inflation-adjusted increases were rarely forthcoming. The Smithsonian Institution's expansion plans were halted, leaving hundreds of items collecting dust in storage rooms far from Americans' view; for years, a historic SR-71 Blackbird supersonic spy plane sat on an Air Force tarmac because the national museum couldn't afford to spend $100,000 to house it. Even once favored programs were starved for funds; for example, for nearly a decade, NASA ran on auto pilot as its share of the budget remained flat, and at one point declined, as a percentage of federal outlays. In the meantime, NASA was expected to complete many new assignments.

Personnel also have been hit hard. Most agencies lost staff during the 1980s. Between fiscal 1982 and 1988, for instance, the General Services Administration was scaled back 43 percent, the Tennessee Valley Authority by 35 percent, and the Education Department by 32 percent. Total, nonpostal, nonmilitary personnel decreased 5 percent between 1982 and 1988, a loss of 60,000 work years.[37]

Decreased Federal Budgets;
Increased Responsibilities

Federal budgets have stalled and even been cut, yet the responsibilities of agencies have in many cases only grown greater. Illegal immigration grows virtually unchecked along the nation's southern border; thousands of new chemicals, their impact on humans unknown, are introduced to products annually; homelessness rises as affordable housing declines; air traffic overloads the skies as cars clog the highways—the list seems depressingly endless.

Even when agencies do get additional resources, work loads still outstrip their capacity to meet responsibilities. The EPA, created in 1970, presides over thousands of regulations governing everything from pesticides to asbestos, and toxic waste to water quality. Its staff size increased 12 percent between fiscal 1982 and 1988, but the agency's critical shortage of environmental engineers and other specialized staff has forced it to contract out many of its expanding responsibilities. This has led to delays in many programs, including Superfund, the government's effort to cleanup the nation's worst toxic waste dumps. Public and private sector organizations have criticized the slow pace of EPA's cleanup activities and warned that it could take EPA several decades to close and render safe most of the dumps.

Other agencies are also experiencing growing demands that contrast considerably with their resources. One telling, even ironic, example is OMB, which employed 769 people at the height of its Nixon-era expansion. By the end of the 1980s, however, OMB employed just 525 people, a handful more than its predecessor, the Bureau of the Budget, had in 1948. In the meantime, the federal budget grew from $30 billion in fiscal 1948 to $1.3 trillion in fiscal 1990. As a result, OMB is unable to give more than a cursory review to many programs—hundreds of which were created in the past 40 years; OMB's management office, which employed roughly 200 people in 1970, had about 40 civil servants remaining by the end of the 1980s—hardly enough to begin grappling with government's deep-seated management practices.

Even the mighty Pentagon has had its problems, though its 40 percent real growth in budget during the Reagan era gained the Defense Department little sympathy from smaller, poorer domestic siblings. Nonetheless, starting in 1985 the Pentagon's budget turned downward, declining 11 percent in real terms by 1989. Not only was the Pentagon forced to stretch out major weapons procurements planned for the 1980s into the 1990s, but it also has caused repair backlogs to rise and research spending to fall. "[The military budget] is very tight when it comes to protecting a force of high quality," Adm. William J. Crowe Jr., then chairman of the Joint Chiefs of Staff warned in 1989. "You will find military compensation falling short of inflation rates, declining investments in equipment modernizations, smaller inventories of spare parts, more deferral of depot maintenance and a growing shortfall of base facility maintenance."[38]

Agencies Shortchanged—Their Impact on Other Services

Consider other agencies shortchanged during the Reagan antigovernment crusade and their impact on federal services:

- The Coast Guard, burdened with increasing drug interdiction responsibilities, reduced its personnel in the late 1980s to digest several years' worth of stagnant or reduced appropriations. Moreover, the agency's fuel and spare parts budget dried up, which ironically grounded planes and pilots that had geared up to fight the administration's war on drugs; boat patrols off the Florida coast were cut in half in 1988 at the same time Reagan was proclaiming a "zero tolerance" policy against drug smuggling.
- By fiscal 1989, in fact, the Coast Guard was operating at pre-1972 personnel levels. Most of the department's other duties were de-emphasized. The Coast Guard's time-honored search and rescue missions received less attention, and its navigation assistance was cut back on heavily traveled oil tanker routes, such as the one in Prince William Sound, Alaska, where the Exxon *Valdez* in 1989 spilled 11 million gallons of crude oil.

- Government statistics, once unchallenged for their accuracy and predictive value, lost both attributes, economists complain. The usefulness of government figures declined as budgets and personnel were cut at the nation's statistical agencies, including the Bureau of Labor Statistics, Bureau of the Census and Bureau of Economic Affairs. Agencies' statistical methodology has not remained current, and the government has fallen behind in its ability to analyze new areas of the country's economy. American companies, which once relied on federal statistical information to make business decisions, have largely turned to private sector experts.

- A 22 percent cut in personnel during the 1980s also took its toll at the Department of Health and Human Services. Cuts at the Health Care Financing Administration reduced that agency's work force by 20 percent during the 1980s at the same time radical changes to Medicare and Medicaid programs were being made; this slowed the transition between old and new medical policies relied upon by millions of Americans. Meanwhile, the Social Security Administration, which manages the government's largest domestic program, lost 17,000 of its 80,000 employees during the decade. The American Federation of Government Employees recently charged that staff at the SSA was reduced 27 percent between 1985 and 1991—at the same time the population served by the agency increased by approximately 10 percent.

Growing Demands and Dwindling Resources

Growing demands and dwindling resources, predictably, have produced delay and inefficiency. Examples from a long list include:

- The backlog of patent applications at the Patent and Trademark Office grew, upwards of four years for biotechnology reviews, during the 1980s, as did corporate filings with the Securities and Exchange Commission.
- The Library of Congress has a backlog of 40 million items waiting to be cataloged. A new item is received every five seconds, every workday of every year.

- The time required for processing some mortgage loans at the Department of Housing and Urban Development has gone from months to years, a delay so excessive that business conditions often had materially changed when approvals came.
- Delays at U.S. Customs and Immigration and Naturalization Service border stations have steadily grown as fewer inspectors encountered increasing numbers of travelers. Massive airport jams have prompted complaints as summer travelers waited as long as five hours to pass through immigration. The story is much the same at border inspection stations: Work loads have risen more than 10 percent annually in the past several years—without almost any increase in staff.

Reagan's Wins and Losses

By the end of the decade, Reagan had both won and lost in his efforts to turn government back to the past. He won, in that dozens of federal agencies had been starved of funds and people. They were indeed weaker, as he had promised in his campaign for the presidency. Agencies during the 1980s atrophied, their capacity and resources, and often their will and morale, sapped. A vote for Ronald Reagan did get government off the backs of the people—but even more, it left government lying on the floor.

But Reagan also lost. For one, his resolve to leave behind a smaller, financially stronger government never materialized. Reagan created a new Cabinet Department and failed—although he had promised—to shut down the Energy and Education Departments, the Small Business Administration, and other agencies. And throughout his two terms, try as he might, Reagan managed to eliminate just two big federal programs: General Revenue Sharing and Urban Development Action Grants. In the process, Reagan tripled the federal deficit, leaving a legacy not easily lived with.

Where Reagan truly lost, however, was in trying to roll America back to the mythical past of his memory. He was wrong. His America—at least how he believed government operated—never existed. Washington in the 1950s taxed, legislated, and protected a nation living in the 1950s; and a nation 30 years later, struggling through the 1980s, needed a government that could do its job, from overseeing a $5.8 trillion economy to managing national security in a multipolar world. Anything less was hollow government.

Chapter 3

The Capitol Circus

T ed Sampley arrived at the Vietnam Veterans Memorial on Columbus Day in 1990 to discover a weekend's worth of garbage strewn about the normally immaculate expanse of grass that stretches from the Capitol to the Lincoln Memorial in Washington, D.C. National Park Service cleanup crews were missing, so Sampley, chairman of the National Steering Committee for American War Veterans, and a group of volunteers spent several hours collecting about 100 bags of trash.[1]

It was the weekend the federal government had shut down.

SHUTDOWN OF THE GOVERNMENT

President Bush, unable to conclude a budget deal with Congress, had refused to sign another stopgap spending measure to keep the government running until Congress and the White House could agree on a budget to fund government operations for the fiscal year that was already under way.

Instead, Bush had closed down federal facilities and offices for three days, telling all civil servants to stay home. As a result, in Washington the monuments were unstaffed. The National Zoo was shut (although its animals were fed), and tourists could only gaze through locked doors at the Air and Space Museum. Around the country, entrance booths at national parks were left unattended—meaning fees went uncollected.

Today, federal agencies have become little more than pawns in a massive chess game between the president and the Congress. Both branches have their own political needs, their own bases of power, their own agendas. A great divide was created between the legislature and the executive in the

American Constitution. It has long been evident in the conduct of presidents and Congresses: Abraham Lincoln's insistence on holding the union together when southern states and their legislatures revolted; Lincoln's vision of a forgiving reconstruction ignored by a revengeful Congress; the civil rights agenda of John Kennedy and Lyndon Johnson colliding with powerful, segregationist senators in control of key congressional committees.

The Responsibilities of the President and Congress

The president is the only elected official with the entire nation as his constituency. As the country's chief executive, the president runs the executive branch; his responsibility is to see that the agencies operate efficiently and equitably, ideally with as little cost as possible. Of course, the president's own parochial concerns get pushed as the White House attempts to implement campaign promises and pay back supporters.

The unique role of U.S. presidents in foreign policy tends to reinforce their homogenous view of America. Many presidents, when faced with the multitude of legislators' local interests inherent in domestic affairs, have tended to focus on international affairs. On the global stage, presidents can more decisively control events, avoiding the myriad regional and fractious issues dominating democracy's deliberative process.

Congress, with 535 men and women eager to prove their worth to the folks back home, cares little about the rational administration of government services. Their interest is distribution—the more federal largesse the better. Lawmakers regularly call on the agencies for a whole range of services, from cutting red tape to extending grants, loans, and even jobs. It is Congress's interest to spread government and its services to as many parts of the country as possible.

"A House Divided"

For all its defense against tyranny, the separation of powers has often confounded the country. And this constitutional dichotomy in recent decades has become more complicated as a result of Washington's politically divided government. Since the mid-1950s, it has been almost exclusively true that the Congress and the White House have been controlled by different parties. For only brief periods of time has any president's party controlled the Congress as well. This schism of power often blunted national leadership.

Since World War II, the United States has had an increasingly polarized, fragmented political system. Only one Democrat, Jimmy Carter, has been president since 1969, and there is much evidence to suggest that his tenure was an aberration, more a result of Republican mistakes (i.e., Watergate and Gerald Ford's pardon of Richard Nixon) than of Democratic strengths.

Opposing parties have controlled one or both houses of Congress and the White House in 26 of the last 38 years. Divided government occurred just 14 percent of the time between 1897 and 1954. But between 1955 and 1990, the country has seen its political house divided 67 percent of the time; since 1969, 80 percent of the time.[2]

Policy stalemates are common. Partisan or parochial issues typically hamper the nation's business. The 1990 budget gridlock is but one example. It precipitated the government's shutdown and even featured a wholesale rejection by Congress's rank and file of their leadership's initial attempt to craft a budget compromise with the Bush administration. For days, Democrats and Republicans argued over the role of tax breaks to the rich (a White House and Republican priority) and the size of domestic spending cuts affecting the poor and middle class (chiefly a concern of the Democrats).

The difficulties of divided government perhaps are most dramatically seen in Richard Nixon's impoundment efforts in the early 1970s. The president became so angry with constantly expanding, expensive Democratic programs that he blocked billions of dollars worth of congressional appropriations by directing executive branch agencies not to spend the funds. Congress, in turn, was so incensed with Nixon's attempt to frustrate its spending power that, in 1974, it passed the Budget and Impoundment Control Act, a law that presidents ever since have blamed for increasing the deficit.

BUDGET BATTLES

The differences inherent in divided government ultimately led parties unable to agree on spending priorities to pass the Balanced Budget and Deficit Reduction Act of 1985, better known as Gramm-Rudman. From across the divide of parties, amidst the conflicting spending goals of legislators, came a law that changed the course of congressional budgeting, by taking the process away from the politicians.

Aaron Wildavsky, one of the most astute observers of the federal budget process, writes that with this single act Congress admitted that its own powers of the purse, its institutional mandate, could no longer be carried out. "The imposition of a formula for replacing the power of the purse, the most important Congressional power, is an abdication of power. Congress is saying that it is out of control."[3]

The Gramm-Rudman Law

In abdicating its 200-year-old responsibility for spending decisions, Congress was admitting in essence that the legislators' priorities continued to be focused on constituency matters and ever growing social programs rather than on the efficient operations of the federal government. With Gramm-Rudman, legislators hoped to control their fiscal frenzy which had seen Democrats seeking to restore Reagan-era cuts to social programs, Republicans pushing for more defense spending, and both parties trying to parcel out jobs and services to their districts.

It has not worked. Agencies, as a result, have been stretched ever thinner, with their limited resources dispersed across many more projects and places. Congress continues to spend more money than it has. Even with tax increases in fiscal years 1982, 1983, 1984, 1987, and 1990, Congress spent more than the Treasury raised. It should surprise no one that the federal budget deficit in fiscal 1992 tops a stunning $360 billion, a record amount of red ink. Despite all the belt-tightening measures that Congress has devised, federal budget outlays in fiscal 1991 represented 25 percent of GNP, the highest since 1946, when federal spending was retreating from World War II records.

Gramm-Rudman required that Congress in its annual budget cycle meet prescribed budget targets designed to eliminate the federal deficit. In order to meet the targets, Congress had to find enough spending cuts and tax increases to reduce the deficit each year. The pressure to curtail spending each year was considerable, because automatic, across-the-board cuts in virtually all government programs were supposed to take effect if the annual deficit target was unmet. For example, in fiscal year 1990, had Congress and the president not finally reached agreement on a compromise budget, Gramm-Rudman would have triggered cuts of 30 percent or more for domestic programs and 40 percent for military programs.

Myopia always has been one of Gramm-Rudman's biggest problems. In mandating annual deficit targets, it sees nothing in the budget beyond the 12-month period of any fiscal year. The long-term investment in the future is shunted aside in the scramble to squeeze under the current year's targets. The budget process shifts from the allocation of scarce resources to merely playing a numbers game. If budget proposals contain long-term savings, but short-term costs, Congress is inclined to forgo those savings to protect themselves from Gramm-Rudman's heavy ax.

For example, in fiscal 1989, by trimming 750 staff-years from work time at the Internal Revenue Service, Congress came up with a $12 million budget "savings." The only problem was that the cut ended up costing the U.S. Treasury more than $100 million in uncollected revenue in future years. Avoiding cuts to federal agencies that collect revenues has a certain elementary logic, but Congress never exempted the IRS from Gramm-Rudman's deficit-reduction formula.

Gramm-Rudman also destroyed much of the rationality, however limited, that once guided Congress's choices in funding public programs. The favorite programs, which traditionally all received additional funds annually, suddenly were competing for dwindling dollars; the focus shifted from program substance to budget impact. At times, the grab for funds gets ludicrous, as legislators reach for relatively unprotected dollars to further pet projects without regard for the impact their actions have on Washington's provision of basic services—or on the management of government. For example, in fiscal 1990, the House Appropriations Committee attempted to secure more than $16 million for pork barrel projects at five universities from the salaries of managers at the General Services Administration, the federal agency responsible for real estate and procurement for the entire government. The plan backfired when a Senate Appropriations Subcommittee objected to the fiscal foolishness.

The competition has spread even among factions on the same committees. For example, the House Appropriations Subcommittee with responsibility for budgets at the Department of Housing and Urban Development and independent agencies such as the Environmental Protection Agency (EPA) and the National Aeronautics and Space Administration (NASA) has found its different interests fighting over scarce resources. Suddenly, more for the EPA or the Department of Veterans Affairs has meant less for NASA. In the fiscal 1991 budget battle, for instance, committees virtually wiped out the president's request for space programs, particularly initiatives for visiting the moon and Mars. The same legislators added billions for housing, the environment, and veterans' care. Congress can't even be consistent in its divided loyalties; one year later, in fiscal 1992, appropriators took money from housing programs and gave it back to NASA.

Common Practice for the Lobbyists

No longer do all agencies benefit from growing budgets and increased appropriations. Strict spending limitations given to appropriations committees have set competing interests against each other in the struggle to keep their funds safe. And so, it has become common practice for the legions of lobbyists, the interest groups surrounding the Capitol, to suggest other parts of the federal budget that could be cut in order to fund the projects they promote. Supporters of the funds under siege then counterattack, and the battle rages. The result is "parasitic" budgeting, a process far removed from the rational, deliberative process accounting for priorities usually associated with budgeting. In the fiscal 1992 fight to fund the NASA's space station, for example, environmentalists, scientists, veterans, and other groups attacked the orbiting platform in an attempt to capture for their own interests the $2 billion in appropriations NASA wanted to keep the station's construction on schedule.

Some spending attacks stage a wider offensive, attempting to draw in money from all types of programs. In the fiscal 1991 appropriations process, a Senate committee responsible for health, labor, and education was constrained by a tight spending limit. The committee drafted a spending bill that provided $2 billion for AIDS research in 1991, but provided no funding at all for AIDS care legislation that had already been signed by President Bush. Angry Senators tried to amend the bill by adding $190 million for the ignored program, but they did so in a manner that produced a storm of protest from advocates of dozens of other equally hard-pressed areas: Legislators tried to cut almost one percent from all proposed spending increases for education, research, and health programs to free money for the AIDS allocation.

Even such seemingly small cuts to the bill would affect the education funding for thousands of elementary school children, and reduce the maximum amount of Pell Grants for poor college students. Rational budgeting is largely gone from the appropriations process, replaced by a funding scramble making it all but impossible for agencies to plan for programs or to even hire new staff.

Indeed, as austerity has touched most domestic programs, legislators have been less able to take credit for new programs, a traditional reelection boost. Although the funds are for the most part no longer available for Congress to shell out to all manner of needy interests, this has not stopped legislators from *pretending* to pass out money. Congress increasingly authorizes billions for new programs, but ends up appropriating just a fraction of the promised funds.

Housing programs, Head Start, even the much-vaunted War on Drugs, are among the many congressional sleights of hand which have received considerably less federal funding than promised in the past few years. Government looks like it is responding to problems (when it really isn't) and expectations among interest groups and constituents are raised when authorizing committees announce new services and more money for programs that, eventually, will barely be funded. The demand for agencies's services rises but the funding doesn't. This game is great for Congress, which can take credit for starting new programs without having to spend much money. Meanwhile, it is the agencies that often get stuck explaining to the bewildered public that funds for newly authorized programs don't exist. The public, in turn, concludes that politics and an inert bureaucracy have denied them their "rights."

BUDGET CAPS

By 1990, even the charade of Gramm-Rudman no longer worked. The federal deficit, for all the political sound and fury devoted to it by politicians, had not decreased by the time Congress turned its attention to the budget for fiscal 1991. A deteriorating economy meant less revenue than had been projected was flowing into the U.S. Treasury. Combined with the hangover of the rising costs of the savings and loan (S&L) bailout, Washington's deficit projections seemed to grow almost monthly.

Congress had hit a brick wall with Gramm-Rudman. The gap between the estimated deficit and the target deficit was too great (about $100 billion too great) for Congress to offer up its usual collection of smoke and mirror savings. Congress faced the choice of ordering an unprecedented multibillion cut to government services or changing the Gramm-Rudman rules. Congress changed the rules.

The Budget Enforcement Act, 1990

Congress approved the Budget Enforcement Act as part of the fiscal 1991 budget package—after months of wrangling with the White House, the Columbus Day weekend shutdown of the government, and the rank and file's rejection of its own leadership's initial agreement with the administration on spending cuts and tax increases.

Gone were Gramm-Rudman's fixed deficit-reduction targets. In their place, Congress wrote in a series of spending caps for discretionary spending programs, set up a pay-as-you-go approach to funding new entitlements, and required that new tax increases offset any new tax cuts.

The practical effect of the Budget Enforcement Act has been to change the focus of budgetary politics from cutting the deficit to cutting spending. The 1990 law divides discretionary spending into three distinct categories: domestic, international, and military. Funds for a fixed period can no longer be transferred from one account to another. Now, Democrats are unable to boost social spending, for instance, by raiding defense accounts. Nor can the total dollars appropriated in any account exceed its budget cap without triggering cuts to all the funds in that category.

For all its noble intention to cut the deficit, the budget agreement allowed outlays to rise 12.6 percent in fiscal 1991, more than twice the rate of inflation, at the same time taxes were raised for the rich and for gasoline and alcohol. Quite simply, the Bush administration bought off Congress by agreeing to higher outlays up front in exchange for future spending restraint.

If Congress honors the new caps, then total federal spending should fall sharply as a share of gross national product. In fact, the government could be back in the black by 1996. There is no guarantee that Congress will keep its word, however. The fiscal 1991 deal is reminiscent of the 1982 budget accord. That year, Congress promised three dollars in outlay reductions for every dollar of tax increases. But in 1983, Congress ignored the promise to cut spending after it got the tax increase.

President Bush, now looking toward his reelection, already has begun discussions with Congressional leaders about breaking the barrier that prevents raiding the defense budget for domestic needs. With the demise of the Soviet Union, even the Pentagon has been scaling back its funding requests (before Congress does it for them), which means that billions of dollars could be freed for other projects. Unfortunately, Bush and many other presidential contenders propose using the quick cash to offer middle-class tax breaks rather than more responsibly devoting the money to either cutting the deficit or supporting beleagured federal agencies and public services.

There are other reasons to be suspect of the fiscal 1991 budget agreement's sanctity. The historically high level of federal outlays it sanctioned could form the beachhead for future program growth. In the U.S. budget process, the current year's spending levels regularly become the baseline from which the following year's outlays are calculated.

Moreover, the Budget Enforcement Act all but precluded the government from turning to traditional fiscal stimulants (i.e., tax cuts and public works programs) to jump start the nation's economic stall in 1991. Even attempts to extend unemployment benefits for out-of-work Americans would break the budget agreement unless the president declared an emergency that allowed that the extra spending not be counted in the budget limitation—which he ultimately did. Thus, for perhaps the first time since Congress passed the Employment Act of 1946 which required the government to emphasize jobs and economic growth in its annual fiscal deliberations, Washington mainly has sat on the sidelines while Americans lost their jobs and businesses.

MANAGING THE GOVERNMENT

Though Congress's budget options are now more limited than they were just two years ago, lawmakers still spend an inordinate amount of time on budget matters. Today, more than 50 percent of the roll call votes in Congress are related to the federal budget or the deficit. Budget and deficit problems, combined with legislators' increasing focus on campaign fundraising, has left Congress with less opportunity to oversee government's management. The result: poorly administered programs, hollow agencies, and an unprecedented amount of federal fraud, waste, and abuse.

Congress reacted late to virtually all of the major government scandals and management mistakes of the 1980s, including the Pentagon procurement abuses, the housing program fraud at the Department of Housing and Urban Development (HUD), and the massive financial losses in the savings and loan industry. Congress ignored early warnings of problems in each of these areas, not even holding hearings until the media were portraying the misdeeds as full-blown scandals.

Congress's Lack of Attention to Priorities

Congress isn't overseeing agencies as it once did. Contrary to popular belief, there are fewer congressional committees and subcommittees now than at any other time in the past 15 years. What's more, the panels that do exist hold fewer hearings than they used to. In the last Congress, the 101st in the nation's history, there were 295 committees and subcommittees, compared with 385 in the 95th Congress of 1975 and 1976. Similarly, committee sessions hit a high of 4,265 in the 94th Congress (1973–74), then declined to 2,493 in the 100th Congress (1987–88).[4]

The inability of Congress to catch fraud and abuse among Pentagon contractors, at HUD, and in the S&L industry has prompted some experts to suggest that the lawmakers reexamine their priorities. "There is some sense that Congress is fiddling while Rome is burning," says Louis Fisher, senior specialist in American National Government at the Congressional Research Service. "Congress is not a good self-starter, [but that] doesn't excuse [committees] for being passive. . . . The banking committees should have been more embarrassed" about the development of the S&L crisis, he says.[5]

Congress itself has belatedly reached a similar conclusion. A Senate subcommittee investigating the HUD scandal in 1990 affirmed that Congress tends to concentrate on new policies and programs, leaving existing ones to fend for themselves and go awry.

Most oversight is of the "fire alarm" variety, prompted by a crisis atmosphere in which committees respond to some agency activity or scandal and then disappear once the problem appears solved. Rep. John D. Dingell (D, Mich.) is perhaps the legislature's best known overseer. Often criticized as the first to the fire and the first to leave, he is known for his

"Dingell-grams," the scores of instructions and queries with which he floods agencies as the powerful chairman of the House Energy and Commerce Committee and its Subcommittee on Oversight and Investigations.

Responsible oversight of agency activity is frustrated by the relatively high rate of congressional staff turnover. Most committee staffers in the House of Representatives hold their jobs for fewer than three years, and more than 50 percent of the lawmakers' personal staffs remain in their jobs less than one year.[6]

Unfortunately, even when Congress does pay attention to management problems in the executive branch, not all that much changes. For example, in 1989 and 1990 at the height of the HUD scandal, House and Senate panels held hearings at which scores of people testified about the billions of dollars in losses. But seemingly to little purpose. Two years after the beginning of the congressional inquiries, losses at the Federal Housing Administration were still growing, and auditors were warning that red ink would continue for several more years.

Much of the increased attention Congress pays to the agencies today has more to do with good politics than good government. Notwithstanding a decline in the number of committees and oversight hearings and a leveling off of committee staff in the last decade, the legislature has involved itself in the daily affairs and operational minutiae of agencies more than ever before. Members essentially use executive branch employees as caseworkers for constituent services, and as conduits for favors, pork, and other assistance designed to enhance their incumbent advantage back home. The Defense Department alone, for instance, received nearly 600,000 phone calls for assistance from members and their staffs in 1984, the last year for which data is available.[7]

Micromanagement

Though Congress is clearly not paying enough attention to the issues that matter, the legislature regularly finds time and energy to engage in more politically oriented micromanagement and oversight. Much of it comes down to numbers: With more than 31,000 people toiling on Capitol Hill, Congress is the most heavily staffed legislature in the world. By comparison, Canada, in second place, has fewer than 3,500 legislative employees. In fact, Congress employs more people than do several cabinet departments, including Education, Energy, HUD, Labor, and State.

The growth in members' personal staffs, a fivefold rise in the House and a sixfold increase in the Senate between 1947 and 1987, is clearly responsible for what agency officials complain is a tremendous and time-consuming rise in micromanagement related to constituent services.[8] Many of the additional new staffers work in state and district offices, where they are paid to run interference for constituents caught in the bureaucracy's red tape.

Fewer full committees and subcommittees in Congress have not reduced the level of legislative micromanagement. The reason: There are more chairpersons, a result of 1970s reforms that gave more members a chance for leadership in Congress. No longer does a handful of powerful committee chairmen dominate several panels. But though most of today's chairpeople are eager to exercise authority, continuing budget deficits constrain opportunities to create new programs; and oversight—of the meddling kind—is about the only power these legislators can wield.

Indeed, more and more of these panels have taken up a mission that was once mainly the preserve of the small handful of subcommittees with specific oversight assignments, such as the oversight panels of the House Ways and Means, the House Energy and Commerce, and the Senate Governmental Affairs Committees. This has meant more freewheeling and uncoordinated reviews of tempting agency targets—more Dingell-like fire alarms.

Federal agencies must now answer to a vast array of congressional committees, even though the amount of time they spend at hearings has remained about the same. The Department of Defense, for instance, figures that the time its officials spend under the glare of committee lights has remained steady during the past 15 years, while the number of committees it answers to has nearly tripled.[9] In 1988, 14 full committees and 43 subcommittees held hearings on Pentagon issues, while some 30 committees and 77 subcommittees claim oversight responsibility. Seventy-four committees and subcommittees claim jurisdiction over America's War on Drugs. William J. Bennett, until 1990 the director of the Office of National Drug Control Policy, repeatedly complained about Congress's continuous demands that he appear at committee hearings.

Congressional Demands Create Reams of Paperwork

Proof of congressional meddling can also be found in the paperwork. Most federal agencies, particularly the Pentagon, now strain under tremendous congressional demands to provide reports, develop proposals, and answer queries that often have little to do with the administration of existing programs. Between 1980 and 1988, Pentagon reports to both the House and the Senate, as tracked by the clerk of the House, grew by 224 percent, far faster than any other part of the government, and nearly three times the average growth of other agencies.[10] Moreover, the Pentagon says that a variety of reports, plans, schedules, and certifications not tracked by the clerk of the House reveal that its paperwork burden is even greater than the official numbers indicate. In 1970, during the Vietnam War, annual funding bills mandated just 36 reports from the Defense Department. In 1988, 719 were required, an increase of nearly 2,000 percent.

Congress's Enforcement of Powers Delays Laws

At the same time, an increasing tendency by Congress to enforce its will through legislative deadlines and regulatory requirements has overwhelmed agencies and stalled the implementation of many laws. For a variety of reasons, including the doubts Democratic lawmakers had of the Reagan administration's willingness to faithfully administer the laws, statutory "hammers" have become Congress's tool of choice in the lawmakers' attempt to ensure that regulatory agencies do Congress's bidding.

Clear evidence of congressional micromanagement of federal agencies exists in the growing complexity and amount of technical detail that's written into many statutes. Rather than leaving agencies free to develop regulations to carry out new laws, as was common in the past, Congress now often specifically guides the regulations' content and sets dates for their drafting and implementation.

One problem is that Congress regularly has set up unreasonable timetables for agencies to follow, and then has failed to provide them adequate resources for carrying out the additional responsibilities. Missed deadlines, unenforced laws, unwritten or delayed regulations often result.

The EPA—Hampered by Congressional Control

The Environmental Protection Agency for years has been hit by congressional hammers. Congress included 328 deadlines in the 15 environmental laws it enacted between 1970 and 1980, but only 14 percent of all the tasks it assigned were accomplished by their deadlines—and just 15 percent of the environmental standards were promulgated by their prescribed time. And despite this dubious record, the 1984 amendments to the Resource Conservation and Recovery Act tossed in more than 60 additional deadlines.[11]

The trend shows no signs of slowing. The Clean Air Act Amendments of 1990, some 700 pages of law, contained more than double the number of deadlines and other legislative hammers than were included in the original Clean Air Act in 1970.

Moreover, two decades after Congress ordered the EPA to identify and regulate air pollutants, emission standards for only seven industrial chemicals have been issued.[12] Likewise, the regulation of drinking water laws is seriously backlogged. Rules to control 32 water pollutants, 10 of which are thought to cause cancer, won't be ready until at least 1993, five years after the law was approved.[13]

THE POLITICS OF PORK

Not all of Congress's traditional spending ways have disappeared, despite budgetary constraints. Even in austere times, legislators still find money to fill the pork barrel for the folks back home. More pressing problems get fewer funds, and agencies already struggling to carry out missions get saddled with additional (often unwarranted and unjustified) duties imposed by Congress's most powerful members.

Examples of Pork Barreling

In fiscal 1991 budget deliberations, for instance, a House-Senate conference committee approved a $21 billion energy and water bill that slashed funds for major science projects while adding funds for a variety of public works projects in states represented by powerful committee chairmen.

The Army Corps of Engineers, a perennial favorite of lawmakers, suddenly found itself with an additional $1 billion at session's end in 1990. Sen. Bennett Johnston (D, La.), chairman of the Senate Energy and Water subcommittee, funneled $93 million to the Red River waterway in his home state. Likewise, Sen. Robert C. Byrd (D, W.Va.), chairman of the money-dispensing Appropriations Committee, claimed millions of dollars for water projects in West Virginia. Byrd also captured millions for road maintenance from the Appalachian Regional Commission, whose appropriations ended up triple the request of the president's budget.

Indeed, Byrd's effectiveness in bringing home the pork has become legendary. Since 1989, when he stepped down from the post of Senate majority leader to head the Senate Appropriations Committee, Byrd has captured for West Virginia more than $1 billion in federal funds. This includes a $185 million FBI fingerprint center being relocated from the District of Columbia to generate jobs in Byrd's home state.[14]

Legislators' Popular Pastimes

The attempt by legislators to move federal facilities to their often rural, recession-battered home districts, or to create offices no agency requested, is more than a popular pastime; it's a major part of being in Congress. Though Byrd may be among Congress's most effective pork barrelers, he is far from the only one. For instance, Rep. John P. Murtha (D, Pa.), chairman of the House Defense Appropriations Subcommittee, slipped a $10 million drug intelligence center into the voluminous fiscal 1991 defense appropriations bill. The legislation stipulates that the center, not surprisingly, be located in Murtha's state, Pennsylvania, and his aides have already let it be known that they expect Johnstown, the largest city within the legislator's district, to be the facility's home.[15]

Neither the Drug Enforcement Administration nor the Defense Department, whose appropriations bill contained the funding, had requested the new center. Murtha's drug intelligence center was not given a specific mission to accomplish; it was created even as existing agencies were trying to eliminate overlapping responsibilities and consolidate more than two dozen intelligence operations, many of which were unable to share their computer-generated data.

Agencies Forced to Accept Unwanted Projects

The National Park Service and the General Services Administration regularly are forced to grapple with projects worth millions of dollars that they neither wanted nor requested from Congress. In 1990, for instance, over the objection of the Park Service, Congress earmarked millions of dollars for dozens of projects and acquisitions that have little to do with the agency's traditional mission. When tallied up, Congress appropriated $271 million in new construction funds, more than three times the park service's request.

Similarly, more than one-half of the new construction projects slated for the General Services Administration in fiscal 1991 by the House Appropriations Committee's Subcommittee for the Treasury Department and Postal Service were never requested by the agency. Rather, many powerful legislators, including then-House Majority Whip William H. Gray III (D, Pa.), and Rules Committee chairman Joe Moakley (D, Mass.) loaded down the appropriations bill with projects directed to their districts, including several projects which had nothing to do with federal buildings.[16]

When it comes to paying for pork, lawmakers are especially attracted to the deep pockets of the Defense Department. Although the Pentagon's budget has dropped since its spending spree in the early 1980s, and will fall further in the post-Cold War era, its $291 billion budget still represents an enticing piggybank for members of Congress eager to please the folks back home.

So intent is Congress on promoting full employment for their constituents that the legislature regularly makes the Pentagon purchase billions of dollars' worth of supplies and weapons that the military doesn't want. Grumman Corp., for instance, the Long Island, New York-based defense contractor, has manufactured weapons for the government since the 1930s, but has lost out in recent bids to build the Pentagon's new generation of jet fighters. The Defense Department repeatedly has told Grumman and Congress that its airplanes are no longer needed, but the region's powerful legislators have kept the unwanted planes coming off production lines for more than a decade.

One of the boldest bows to the power of the pork barrel came in 1990 when Lockheed Corp., winner of the contract to produce the Air Force's new Advanced Tactical Fighter, was so intent in keeping its share of dwindling defense contracts that it moved its aerospace division from California to Georgia, where it could do business under the roof of a powerful senator, Democrat Sam Nunn, chairman of the Armed Services Committee. General Dynamics followed suit in 1991, announcing that it would transfer the corporation's headquarters operation from St. Louis, Missouri, to suburban Washington, D.C., where it presumably could better follow defense procurement issues.

Legislative and Executive Branches Adept at Game Playing

For all of the pressure and manipulation employed by members of Congress to purloin their share of public services, savvy executive branch departments are equally adept at playing the game. And most agencies with big-ticket programs learned long ago that the best way to encourage lawmakers to keep the dollars coming is to share the wealth.

As a result, most of the government's big programs, primarily large weapons and science contracts, are spread out across the country. Lawmakers approve the projects because their district will get part of the action, and then defend them to make sure the jobs or services are not taken away. Wise politically, such activities are unwise from a public management perspective. Indeed, they almost constitute a conflict of interest since members of Congress, eager to protect their share, are unlikely to challenge any of the waste, fraud, and abuse which typically occurs in big price-tag projects. Nor are they willing to cancel the projects and risk losing jobs back home.

A prime example is the government's Superconducting Super Collider. To be built by the year 2000 in Waxahachie, Texas, the SSC (what one congressman terms the *quark barrel*) is an $8.2 billion atom smasher designed to help scientists learn more about the basic building blocks of matter. Yet the Super Collider seems mainly to be more about building orders for business. More than 8,500 contracts have been awarded to companies in 43 states, and all before a single shovelful of dirt has been moved for construction in Waxahachie.[17] Lawmakers and private industry are happy with the deal; meanwhile, the Department of Energy's estimates for the collider's costs continue to rise along with the federal deficit.

Another pork project is the $38 billion space station. When the NASA program in 1991 was almost eliminated by House appropriators facing tight budgets, the space agency rushed to Capitol Hill. Neither the quest for science nor American leadership in space were the primary arguments used to convince reluctant legislators. Instead, NASA highlighted the number of jobs, about 100,000 in 40 states, that would be lost if the station were canceled. No surprise, it wasn't canceled.

Budget Cuts in Share-the-Wealth Projects

Increasingly, this time-honored method for encouraging reelection is clashing with the overall needs of a nation struggling to streamline an often outdated federal structure and to eliminate the deficit. No longer can public funds—in the form of jobs and bureaus, parks, military bases, and hospitals—be handed out to every state and district as part of an ever-growing federal scheme to spread the wealth and ensure favored budget treatment.

Austerity and a growing deficit, changing demographics and a shrinking military have, for the first time in years, shifted the budget's balance. Agencies are seeking to cut costs through consolidating field offices, the Pentagon is closing domestic military bases as Communism crumbles, and the Department of Veterans Affairs, burdened with 172 mostly northern hospitals, is trying to provide services for an aging veterans' population today mainly living in the Sunbelt.

Unfortunately, Congress is not equal to the task. Legislators are all for trimming budgets and cutting back, as long as it doesn't include their district. Thus, Congress is happy to open new VA hospitals, but isn't interested in shutting down old ones. Even a proposal to study how the system could be better streamlined has been blocked by lawmakers. The result: VA is forced to operate more facilities with limited resources, which in turn reduces both the quantity and quality of its care to veterans.

Political Parochialism

Political parochialism ranges from preventing the U.S. Coast Guard from closing underutilized stations in New Jersey during the late 1980s, at the same time it had no funds for fuel to operate some anti-narcotics aircraft, to the Federal Bureau of Investigation being ordered to keep open unneeded offices in Montana when it couldn't provide enough special agents to handle the growing number of bank fraud cases in the Southwest. And the Department of Agriculture, the faltering voice of a once powerful constituency, is forced to keep the lights on in an astounding 15,000-plus offices worldwide. Meanwhile, USDA's Agricultural Stabilization and Conservation Service has not been granted the resources to handle new wetlands responsibilities under the 1985 and 1990 Farm Acts, and the Food and Nutrition Service remained understaffed in its administration of nutrition programs for disadvantaged Americans.

Still, nothing surpasses the high stakes legislators face in closing military bases. The potential loss of thousands of military and civilian jobs and the attendant economic consequences to a lawmaker's district has literally kept Congress from voting on the issue. Military base closings are so volatile that, just as with budget deficit agreements, Congress has put the difficult decisions, and with it the accountability, on autopilot. Legislators craftily created a base closings plan that keeps their fingerprints off the painful cuts. Indeed, the base closings, picked by a special commission, not legislators, are designed to occur unless Congress specifically votes to cancel the entire package. Politically spineless though it is, this method of closing bases has generally worked.

Nonetheless, this approach apparently has limited utility, as Veterans Affairs Secretary Edward Derwinki discovered in 1990. Encouraged by the success of the base closings commission, Derwinski tried to interest Congress's veterans affairs committees in creating a similar structure to downsize the department's outmoded hospital system. Powerful veterans' groups complained to Congress, however, and the idea was killed, leaving the Veterans Administration (VA) no way to make more efficient use of its resources.

P A R T

II

HOLLOW GOVERNMENT

W ithout support from its people and attention from its elected leaders, government suffers. Only in recessions and as a last resort do the nation's brightest individuals consider government careers. With no payback in votes and political mileage, legislators ignore government's management. The quality of the Washington work force and its physical infrastructure decline as an ever distrustful citizenry decides through its politicians that there has been enough of "government growth." Pay raises to attract quality employees and investments for modern equipment, or even maintenance, are deferred in the name of deficit reduction. Demands are placed on agencies without regard to the resources needed. Responsibilities critical to effective program management are parceled out to the private sector. Finally, an ever changing cycle of leaders determined to work their will on an allegedly unresponsive public service inject political influence into professional decision making, at times undermining laws, and often ignoring those most qualified to shape public policy.

Part II examines the impact of persistent federal disinvestment and the erosion of the public's regard for government at a time when demands for federal services continue expanding.

Chapter Four, "The Last Resort," discusses Uncle Sam's increasing problems in attracting and retaining a quality work force. The result of disinvesting in people has been, and will continue to be, deteriorating taxpayer services and program effectiveness.

Chapter Five, "The Management Mess," looks at the effect budget austerity and misplaced priorities have had on the government's physical infrastructure and management. From outmoded computers to archaic accounting systems, deteriorating buildings to equipment shortages, management neglect has hampered, even prevented, the efficient use of tax dollars.

"Shadow Government" is reviewed in Chapter Six. Thousands of private companies now do much of the work the government has historically done itself. Many wind up making public policy decisions, an undeniably inappropriate role for profit-seeking firms. In turn, agencies are ill-equipped to make decisions themselves.

Chapter Seven, "Aiding America," details the impact of Hollow Government on the provision of state and local services. This chapter looks at the cutbacks in federal aid for cities and states, for streets and public works, and the impact such disinvestment will have on the country.

Chapter Eight, "Inside Agencies," briefly examines the impact of Hollow Government on several agencies. The Department of Housing and Urban Development, the Internal Revenue Service, the Consumer Product Safety Commission, and the National Park Service are classic examples of agencies whiplashed by increasing demands and shrinking or stagnant resources.

Chapter Four

The Last Resort

A decade ago, Paul Volcker received some interesting mail. Arguably the second most powerful person in the country—second only to Jimmy Carter and Ronald Reagan, the presidents who successively appointed him—Volcker was receiving bricks and two-by-fours from angry construction workers around the country.

VOLCKER AND THE FEDERAL RESERVE SYSTEM

Volcker was chairman of the Board of Governors of the Federal Reserve System, and in the late-1970s and early-1980s the "Fed" was keeping a tight lid on the nation's money supply to try to contain boiling inflation. Since people tend not to buy houses when money is tight, new home construction suffers. Thus, the mailed protests of bricks and two-by-fours.

Not long after declining Reagan's offer for a third term at the helm of the Fed, Volcker became chairman of another important organization. This time, construction workers and the general public remained largely ignorant of its existence—even though the work of the National Commission on the Public Service was of critical importance. Its ambitious task was to advance solutions for fixing a badly damaged federal work force.

The Volcker Commission—A Quiet Crisis

The panel, informally dubbed the Volcker Commission, issued a report in 1989 that captured more than a decade of mounting frustration on the part of people working for Uncle Sam. Indeed, so dispirited had the civil service become that by the mid-1980s, a "quiet crisis" was said to underlie the dismal relationship between the bureaucracy and its employer.

This was no union feud with management. To be sure, the civil service wanted—and after years of neglect deserved— higher pay, better health benefits, and other perks for which unions typically fight. In no small measure, however, what America's public servants really wanted was respect. The nation's growing lack of confidence in its government was conferred by proximity, if not by deed, on its federal workers. The prime-time disdain leveled at both government and the professional bureaucracy by Richard Nixon, Jimmy Carter, and Ronald Reagan only made matters worse.

Since the 1970s the quiet crisis has steadily grown louder. College graduates have found better paying jobs in the private sector, especially during the economic boom of the 1980s, that carry none of the bureaucracy's stigma. As the country increasingly identifies government as a cause, instead of a solution, of society's problems, many of the civil service's brightest employees have departed for the country's colleges and corporations.

The Volcker Commission summed up the quiet crisis well: "It is evident that public service is neither as attractive as it once was nor as effective in meeting perceived needs. No doubt, opposition to the specific policies of government has contributed to a lack of respect for the public servants who struggle to make the policies work. This drives away much of our best talent which can only make the situation worse."[1]

The problems of serving in government today are many. Federal pay and benefits often lag well behind private sector compensation. Drug testing requirements and ethics rules are demeaning and smack of distrust, and critical professional needs such as travel and training often are denied as agency budgets tighten. For those who answer the government's call, most quickly find their advancement stymied by the increasing politicization of the career civil service.

WORKING FOR WASHINGTON

To say that Uncle Sam can't find anyone to hire, or that no one wants to work for the government, isn't quite right. After all, the federal government hired about 130,000 people in 1990.[2]

Indeed, plenty of people work for the government: About 2.1 million civilian employees, another 775,321 postal workers, and 1.9 million uniformed military personnel.[3] In fiscal 1992 Washington will spend nearly $219 billion for the bureaucracy's personnel costs.[4]

Shortage of Applicants for Government Jobs

In many cases, however, the government simply is not hiring the people it wants, nor enough of them. Hundreds of civil service jobs, particularly high-level career positions, go unfilled because the government cannot find qualified people to fill them. Federal agencies have had an especially tough time getting enough qualified scientists and engineers, doctors and nurses, law enforcement officials, lawyers, statisticians, and accountants.

What's more, because similar shortages often exist in the more lucrative private sector, when the government does successfully recruit people, it frequently ends up with less-qualified individuals—even those workers rejected by industry. In short, government is the employer of last resort, often receiving the country's least qualified and motivated applicants.

After compiling a survey of 1988 college graduates, the Volcker Commission offered this sobering conclusion: "Few of the top graduates feel the federal government can offer good pay and recognition for performance. Fewer still say a federal job can be challenging and intellectually stimulating.[5] This worrisome trend even has taken hold among graduates of public administration programs, specifically those young people trained for government jobs. Many are increasingly disinclined to consider civil service employment: 25 percent fewer graduates of such programs joined the federal government between 1979 and 1988.[6]

It is becoming more common to encounter negative views of public service among recent college graduates. For example, more than 70 percent of the graduates surveyed by the Volcker Commission stated that responsibility is difficult to obtain early in a federal career; roughly half said that government jobs are routine and monotonous; almost 80 percent said civil-servants lack the power and opportunity to influence policy; and less than 3 percent said that top government jobs could be reached through the civil service.[7]

Examples of Recruiting Problems in Some Agencies

Such dim perceptions have had a clear impact on the government's ability to hire quality recruits and, in turn, on the effectiveness of its services. The employer of last resort has, as a result, encountered troublesome problems with its work force. Consider the following situations:

- The Internal Revenue Service has reported that up to 50 percent of the people who accept jobs never actually show up for their first day of work. They obtain better paying jobs between the time of their IRS offers and their scheduled starting dates with the agency. More-over, the IRS has been unable to attract the brightest graduates, most of whom are aggressively courted by the country's big accounting firms. The IRS has had to hire its revenue agents from the 54th percentile and lower of an American Institute of Certified Public Accountants' examination, compared with candidates scoring in the 86th percentile and higher who are hired by large private accounting firms.
- The Department of the Navy has been unable to recruit its first- or even second-choice candidates for engineering positions. The Naval Sea Systems Command tries to hire individuals with a college grade point average of 2.6 or better, approximately a B−. But with at least one-third of its recent recruits, NavSea was forced to accept graduates with less than 2.6 averages.[8]
- The percentage of medical staff fellows who convert their positions to full-time employment, after spending considerable time working in the government at the still prestigious but resource-strapped National Institutes of Health, has dropped almost in half, from 8.3 percent during 1975–79 to 4.2 percent during 1983–87.[9]

Government's Attitude toward New Recruits

The less-than-sterling quality of new federal recruits is not lost on veteran civil servants. Several recent surveys have indicated that mid- and senior-level managers throughout the federal government consider incoming recruits to be less qualified than previous new employees.

For example, a 1990 *Government Executive* magazine survey of civil servants who had won the government's top awards for distinguished public service showed that 75 percent were concerned that the quality of employees had eroded over previous years.[10]

The Quality of Applicants

Another 1990 survey, this one conducted by the government itself, revealed that for every category of job applicant on which supervisors were questioned, no less than 40 percent perceived a decline in applicant quality over the previous four years; and no more than 25 percent of them saw any improvement in the quality of new employees.[11] Indeed, for most job categories surveyed, a plurality of supervisors in the civil service suggested that the situation had worsened in the previous four years. Fewer supervisors rated the quality of applicants as "somewhat or greatly improved," while the number of bosses claiming quality had "somewhat or greatly worsened" had risen by roughly 10 percentage points since the earlier survey in 1986.

"This is the crux of the 'quiet crisis'—a work force that appears to be slowly declining in quality at a time when the demands being made on it are increasing," reported the U.S. Merit Systems Protection Board, the federal agency conducting the surveys. "The ultimate effects of this combination of events are unsettling to contemplate."[12]

Current Recruiting Problems

The inability to recruit enough qualified people, along with the declining quality of new college graduates that the government *does* hire, has in large measure contributed to an erosion in federal services. By refusing to invest in quality personnel, the government's efficiency and its services suffer. Agencies without adequate, well-trained staff have more difficulties meeting the public's growing demands. Consider these typical examples:

- The Dallas office of the Internal Revenue Service has lost an "unspecified" amount of tax revenues because the heavy work load demands on the agency's attorneys meant that bankruptcy cases were not being pursued.
- Department of Labor officials in New York City relate that difficulties in recruiting industrial hygienists have added to its case backlog and contributed to a decline in the quality of work at its Occupational Safety and Health Administration (OSHA). Specifically, the OSHA offices in Queens and Manhattan have logged fewer inspections and are far behind in achieving their program goals.[13]

Services have especially suffered at the Department of Veterans Affairs as a result of that agency's inability to recruit qualified employees:

- Two wards at the VA's Atlanta hospital were closed in the late 1980s as a result of professional and nursing staff shortages. Both doctors and nurses were performing administrative tasks such as answering phones and copying documents—which meant they were treating fewer patients.[14]
- VA Medical Centers in St. Louis had between 60 and 80 nursing vacancies during a 1990 review by the General Accounting Office. On a recent VA certification inspection, the hospitals there earned the lowest possible rating.
- Medical centers in several other cities also have reported severe recruiting problems, especially for nurses. As a result, hospitals have closed wards and delayed the opening of new facilities, causing crowding and delays in treatment.[15]

Worsening Recruiting Problems in the Near Future

As disturbing as Uncle Sam's current recruiting problems already have become, they are unfortunately bound to worsen. As the baby boomers of the 1960s age and retire, demographers say that there simply will not be enough educated, highly skilled people entering the work force to take their places in the government or industry. Competition for the best and brightest people, a struggle that government has long been losing to the private sector, will only intensify as we enter the 21st century.

Moreover, personnel problems could worsen among the government's professional, white-collar workers. They currently comprise 48 percent of the federal government's employees, compared to about 25 percent for the nation as a whole.[16] Between 1976 and 1986, the government's professional, technical, and administrative ranks grew from 52 percent to 59 percent of the federal work force, while clerical jobs fell from 22 percent to 19 percent, and blue-collar positions declined from 24 percent to 19 percent of the total.[17] Demographers expect these trends to accelerate, and that means there'll be even greater demand among federal agencies for engineers, accountants, and other workers already in short supply.

THE FEDERAL BRAIN DRAIN

The government has difficulties not only in hiring people but also in keeping them. Both recruits and veteran civil servants are heading for the doors.

Government increasingly is serving as a training ground, a place for young college graduates, where in two or three years they acquire the skills they need for more lucrative private sector employment. Fully one-quarter of all employees resign from their jobs within one year of joining the government.[18] At agencies where scarce skills always are in demand—the Environmental Protection Agency, the Internal Revenue Service, the Justice Department, the Federal Communications Commission, and the Securities and Exchange Commission, for example—young people learn the basics, then leave.

Young Employees versus Senior Executives

Accompanying this worrisome and rapid turnover of young people in government is the alarming brain drain of senior federal executives. Most simply are fed up with the conditions under which they must work. Because qualified replacements at top levels are so tough to come by, when these senior civil servants abandon agencies, their jobs often go unfilled for months, even years. The National Institutes of Health were unable to fill one senior science position for most of the 1980s. Also in the mid-1980s, the Naval Research Laboratory could not staff 94 critical scientific and engineering positions.[19]

Unfortunately, the retention situation is about to be made worse. More than 50 percent of all federal employees are between the ages of 36 and 55, and many of them could retire as early as 1994 due to the recent changes in the federal employees' retirement system. Reforms instituted in 1984 make it easier for government workers to leave after 10 years of service, and there is every reason to believe that substantial numbers of experienced personnel will resign as soon as they become eligible for retirement. The U.S. Merit Systems Protection Board states, "unless steps are now taken to retain experienced, retirement-eligible workers in the Federal work force, severe shortages may be inevitable in many occupations."[20]

This concern was underscored by a *Federal Employees' News Digest* survey concluding that 65 percent of the mid- and high-level executives responding said that they would probably retire when they became eligible.[21]

Two years before the potential bailout, it's already clear that a mass exodus of seasoned federal workers is in the making. For instance, at the Internal Revenue Service alone, roughly 70 percent of its top executives are now eligible to retire. The U.S. Government is about to lose a significant portion of its institutional memory—and with it will go many of the means to administer programs and deliver services to people all across the country.

NASA's Loss of Skilled Workers Perils Future Missions

What's worse is that many agencies already haven't the skilled leadership needed to pursue their missions. Both NASA and the Department of Energy have admitted in recent years that their organizations may no longer have the in-house skills and knowledge to do their jobs.

NASA is a perfect example of the situation. Once among the finest technical organizations in the nation, the agency's abilities have been deteriorating since the Apollo program came off the launch pad. NASA's budget and personnel needs were neglected by the White House during most of the 1970s and 1980s, even when new tasks such as the space shuttle, planetary probes, satellites, and space telescopes were thrust upon it. With considerably more work, but with little increase in staff, NASA quickly found itself overburdened. More and more, the agency turned to contractors and, by the mid-1980s, discovered that much of its vital work was being done by the private sector, often by former senior scientists and engineers who had left the space agency to join higher paying government contractors. Indeed, as then-NASA Deputy Administrator James R. Thompson told *The New York Times* in 1989, "I am most deeply concerned over the continued erosion of our civil service capability."

NASA is not alone in the loss of quality employees or agency memory. The numbers of patents earned and research papers produced by scientists at Defense Department laboratories declined markedly between 1958 and 1987.[22] The Department of Energy has seen many of its veteran nuclear research and production employees depart.

Inability to Produce Quality Work Spreads throughout the Government

Concerns over the federal government's inability to do quality work is spreading beyond management to the federal work force in general. A 1989 study revealed that 30 percent of people across the government believed the quality of work their agencies produced could be improved; that constituted a 20 percent increase in the number of people who believed that government quality wasn't all it could be just three years before.[23]

Such statistics should not come as a surprise. Because agencies often are unable to hire experienced outside managers to replace departing senior managers, they are faced more and more with promoting people who would otherwise be passed over. Agencies have been reduced to body snatching in order to try to flesh out their ranks. A representative of the National Weather Service candidly told the Volcker Commission: "We deal with recruiting by stealing from other agencies."[24]

EMPLOYER OF LAST RESORT

A public service career has always required something special from the people who heard its call. No one was likely to become a millionaire by earning a federal paycheck—at least not legally. But the rewards that could only be found in government seemed, for most who sought it, to more than compensate for what the treasury could not. Managers who left the government generally realized that the work done for Uncle Sam could not be found in the private sector. From planning the Apollo moon mission to overseeing the banking industry, the federal government offers challenges and psychic rewards that only the public sector, through its uniqueness, can offer.

The reasons why people join government today and stay with it are basically the same as they always have been. The challenges and the rewards that come with making society better instead of, perhaps, making some detergent better, are still a powerful motivator. But in an age of "bureaucrat-bashing," and when many no longer can afford to stay, these rewards no longer seem to be enough.

Compensation a Main Factor in Work Force Decline

Part of the problem is compensation. A climbing deficit, a politically sensitive Congress unwilling to vote bureaucrats more money, and antipathy toward the government have not been conducive to federal pay raises. Although the public sector has historically lagged behind the private sector's compensation, the situation became noticeably worse starting in the late-1970s. Although a new law in 1970 had attempted to overhaul antiquated federal compensation procedures and to legislate public wages comparable with private sector salaries, its provisions, and decent federal raises, have been ignored most of the time.

The Federal Pay Comparability Act of 1970

The Federal Pay Comparability Act of 1970 required a group of federal officials, including the director of the Office of Management and Budget and the director of the Office of Personnel Management, to each year recommend to the president civil service salary ranges to keep government workers' wages competitive with the private sector. The president, in theory, was to include this recommendation in the federal budget, with the recommended raises to be approved as part of Congress's annual appropriations process.

Great theory, but it almost never happened. In 1972, the pay agent's raise recommendation fell victim to the wage and price controls enacted as part of President Nixon's Economic Stabilization Act. A 6.6 percent recommended raise was pared to 5.5 percent that year, and more reductions soon followed.

For most of its existence, in fact, the law mandating federal pay comparability simply was dismissed. During the 20 years between 1970 and 1990 when the statute was the basis for setting federal salaries, the pay agent's recommendations were adhered to only six times. As a result, between 1978 and 1990 the gap between private and public sector salaries had grown to nearly 30 percent, and for certain hard-to-recruit specialties in the country's highest cost areas, the pay gap often was considerably greater.[25]

Pay Reform Measures

Then Congress and the president approved two pay reform measures as we entered the 1990s—one which provided a nearly 30 percent raise to members of the Senior Executive Service, and another which over the next decade will attempt to make public sector salaries competitive with private industry by increasing federal employees' pay based on geographic living standards.

Though there is considerable optimism that the pay raises will improve the government's ability to recruit and retain higher caliber employees, it will be several years, federal personnel managers say, before the government knows whether pay reform can successfully halt the civil service's decline.

In the meantime, pay reform has inadvertently set the stage for a possible mass exodus in 1994 of the government's most experienced civil servants. During 1989 and 1990, for example, retirement-eligible members of the Senior Executive Service put off their departures in anticipation of the coming salary increases. Under federal retirement rules, pensions are based on a three-year slice of a worker's highest salary rate. Thus, those SESers who postponed retirements, waiting for the 1991 pay raise, will be eligible to receive higher pensions starting in 1994.

Personnel managers at many agencies are seriously concerned about losing large portions (in some cases a majority) of their most experienced, hard to replace senior executives. Replacing them with equally experienced people, from either the private or public sector, will prove very difficult. Keeping a quality work force will continue to be a serious challenge for the federal government.

GOVERNMENT ETHICS

Problems with pay and compensation invariably are linked to federal recruitment and retention difficulties, but they are hardly the only reasons for the growing disillusionment with public service. Strict ethics regulations that prohibit departing federal workers from accepting certain types of jobs, or even from working in their career field for many years, have discouraged experienced private sector managers from joining the government. Many prominent and talented corporate executives undoubtedly share the views of Norman R. Augustine, chairman and chief executive of Martin Marietta Corp., who complained to the Volcker Commission that he had no interest in becoming a test case for what he considered to be vague postemployment restrictions.

The increasing stringency of ethics regulations in recent years has also sparked many civil service resignations. More than a dozen top managers have left NASA and the Department of Energy in the past several years rather than submit to conflict of interest rules restricting their future employment.

Financial Disclosure—A Deterrent to Public Service

Moreover, many of the nation's most successful private citizens now avoid public service because of the extensive financial disclosure information required by the White House as a condition of high-ranking federal employment. Information provided in such instances is available to the public and the press frequently disseminates the material far and wide. Many Americans concerned with families and privacy have, as a result, turned down public service offers.

Not that ethics regulations should be scrapped. They're designed, for instance, to prevent federal workers from being influenced by private sector contractors who promise postgovernment jobs and to halt the spin of the "revolving door"—the phenomenon of federal employees leaving the government for the private sector and its higher salaries, only to return to the government at a more senior position, and then again depart for still higher pay in industry or consulting.

Clearly, it is in Uncle Sam's interest to find a middle ground. To be sure, a revolving door in Washington promotes instability and the notion that government jobs are available for personal aggrandizement. Yet such agencies as NASA, the Defense Department, and the Environmental Protection Agency are harmed by the strict regulations that scare away candidates for their senior positions. Overly strict regulations suggest that federal employees are not to be trusted, especially when only a handful of career and political executives seek to gain unfair personal advantage from their jobs.

Transference of Knowledge and Skills between Public and Private Sectors

What's more, there is much to be gained from transfering knowledge and skills between the private and public sectors. Creating strict walls between government and industry, including federal contractors, denies both sides opportunities to share information and technology and sows distrust and animosity. This is an especially critical point for such technology-driven agencies as the Pentagon, the Energy Department, and the National Institutes of Health. Government has long been criticized for risk-avoidance behavior and organizational stagnation—both situations could be remedied through broader interaction with business, industry, and the rest of the private sector.

IMPACT OF THE QUIET CRISIS

The federal government, monolithic as it seems, is like any other organization in that it requires dedicated and motivated people for its successful operation. The private sector has recognized this fact for years, and many companies work hard to promote and praise their employees.

The nation as a whole loses when the federal government is unable to recruit and retain superior workers. Public service increasingly has been dismissed and disparaged as the popular myth of an incompetent, burgeoning bureaucracy flourishes. Misguided as it is, there even exists one school of thought, embodied in public choice economics, that discourages top graduates from joining the public service. Government, this philosophy basically holds, ought to be run by the mediocre, leaving the best minds free to enhance the nation's gross national product.

Those who would deny government its share of America's best and brightest would erase probes to far-off planets, the isolation of the AIDS virus, the salvage of endangered species, and productive farming in virtual deserts, otherwise known as the American West, to name just a few of the myriad activities civil servants do or support. Advancements in chemistry, biology, medicine, weaponry, energy, and the environment routinely emanate from federal labs and offices. And just as in private industry, the advances and notable achievements are accomplished by talented individuals: the assets of the agencies.

Situations Showing Impact of Lost Personnel

The impact of the federal government's personnel problems can be seen in the decline of dozens of agencies, where missions are downgraded or ignored and where public responsibilities are only undertaken when time and people are available. Consider some of these problems:

- The New York office of the Internal Revenue Service (IRS) has been unable to retain its staff attorneys. Cases are, at best, delayed and often are mishandled by attorneys unfamiliar with the issues because they are taking over someone else's work. For example: It takes a minimum of four years to learn the intricacies of estate taxes, but nearly two-thirds of the attorneys in the IRS New York City office have less than three years' experience. Thus, some of the nation's most sophisticated tax returns and settlements are reviewed by an inexperienced staff, leading to unknown losses resulting from missed tax revenues.[26]

- The high turnover rate of FBI agents and Justice Department lawyers has slowed the investigation and prosecution of thousands of savings and loan fraud cases. Sophisticated fraud cases typically take three or four years to investigate and prosecute, and when experienced supervisors and managers leave the FBI (about 70 percent now are eligible for retirement), preparation slows as inexperienced agents and attorneys unfamiliar with the cases, and sometimes even unfamiliar with bank fraud, take over.

- Turnover has been epidemic at the Environmental Protection Agency, which manages the clean up of the nation's worst toxic waste dumps as part of the Superfund program. Superfund cleanups are big business to private companies vying for federal contracts, and experienced EPA environmental engineers are much in demand. In some parts of the country, Superfund program offices have seen nearly 30 percent of their staff depart annually, and the average turnover is more than 25 percent.[27] And anecdotal evidence suggests that the turnover rate for some technical specialists is higher. The result: cleanups are delayed, and the chance for human harm grows.

- Pharmacists have been extremely difficult to retain at the Veterans Affairs Medical Centers. Several pharmacy operations at VA hospitals have reported problems with slower service delivery, backlogs, and a decline in quality as their most experienced pharmacists depart and fewer quality replacements are found. The potential for prescription error has increased, since inexperienced pharmacists make two to four times as many errors as experienced personnel.[28]

POLITICS AND ADMINISTRATION

The United States is unlike other major industrialized democracies in that a change in presidents brings with it a wholesale change in the government's top ranks. Less than 100 officeholders relinquish their positions when governments change in England or France elects a new president. Yet each time a new president enters the Oval Office, more than 3,000 people across the government are shown the door and approximately an equal number of people are invited to take their places. And it is this latter event (the thousands of people sweeping into senior policy positions) that creates problems for government's management. Certainly many presidential choices are highly regarded in their fields and worthy of the positions to which they are appointed. Nonetheless, many others are friends, financial contributors, and campaign workers being rewarded for their loyalty. To them go the senior-level spoils of victory.

Political Patronage throughout America's History

This is by no means a new phenomenon in America. Rewarding the party and personally faithful has a rich tradition. Though Andrew Jackson's mobocracy remains the pre-eminent example of political patronage at the apex of power, throughout the country's history, even when the government was considerably smaller, a comparatively large number of new bosses were imposed on the permanent bureaucracy with every presidential transition.

Few citizens, even federal employees, would deny incoming presidents the right to appoint people to a whole range of government positions. What has become worrisome, however, is the increase in recent years of purely "political" appointments. Much of the influx stems from presidents determined to work their will over a supposedly uncooperative bureaucracy.

Richard Nixon, Gerald Ford, and Jimmy Carter all pushed more political appointees into the bureaucratic ranks. But it was Ronald Reagan who truly mastered control of the executive branch through close White House supervision of the presidential appointments process. Indeed, Reagan created a sophisticated personnel office more than 10 times the size of the one operated by John Kennedy.

Though presidents from Nixon onward began to pay more attention to filling sub-cabinet jobs with political nominees, only with Reagan did the age-old political patronage tool become a sharp-edged weapon. To effectively create the "Reagan Revolution," every power base in government was to be controlled directly from the White House.

Filling Top Ranks with Antigovernment Personnel

Using loyalty to the president and his conservative agenda as a "litmus test" to be passed by political appointees, Reagan's personnel office frequently filled the top ranks of federal agencies with people philosophically opposed to the government and agencies they administered. In agency after agency, Reagan's personnel apparatus ensured that only those who shared the president's strict antigovernment values would hold critical positions in the federal hierarchy.

Indeed, the substitution of loyalty and narrow agendas for professional judgment and public service is an important but often overlooked reason for the government's problems with morale and quality among its executive ranks. This philosophical- and personnel-driven shift alienated many long-time career executives, and hastened numerous government departures. Reagan, in one administration, did more to politicize the neutral competence of civil servants than any other president in modern history. Political appointees moved deeper than ever before into federal agencies and bureaus. Pendleton James, director of personnel for Ronald Reagan, recalls, "We handled all the appointments: boards, commissions, schedule Cs, ambassadorships, judgeships. . . . We were the first White House in history that selected judges. We made a concerted effort in the planning stages at the very beginning before we became an administration, that if you are going to run the government, you've got to control the people that come into it."[29]

A much politicized executive branch, accentuated under Reagan, actually had been growing for nearly 50 years. Seventy-one positions in the federal government required presidential nominations and Senate confirmations in 1933. By 1985 there were 527 such positions. To be sure, the government has grown considerably at all levels since the time of Franklin Roosevelt. What has increased significantly in recent years, however, is the number of mid-level agency political positions that long had been filled by experienced career veterans.

Expansion of Political Positions a Detriment to Good Management

Today there is growing recognition that the expansion of political positions has negatively affected management of the government and the motivation and morale of the civil service. As more mid-level positions are offered to party loyalists, the buffer grows between experienced program managers and agency heads, diminishing accountability to Congress and the public. Moreover, the layering of political positions deeper in federal agencies cuts off career employees from promotion opportunities, further limiting their incentives to remain in the public service. Such important government positions as deputy assistant secretary, essentially the top-line management jobs, have traditionally been held by career executives with years of federal service. More often than not, these jobs are now off-limits to the people who have spent their careers preparing for them.

Unparalleled politicization of the public service has created problems among civil servants; also there has been a dramatic rise in pressure and delays evident in the White House personnel office, which in turn has often delayed leadership direction for federal departments. Amidst the tone-setting and policymaking, the White House must deal with tens of thousands of letters, phone calls, and personal appeals from jobseekers. Pendleton James reports that at the start of Ronald

Reagan's first presidential term, the White House received about 45,000 letters from people seeking jobs in the new administration. James estimates that he received over 500 job-related letters in a day, compared to approximately 500 letters received in a month by Dan H. Fenn, Jr., John Kennedy's personnel assistant.[30]

Additionally, the burden involved in finding, recruiting, and obtaining security clearances, and in many cases, getting Senate approvals, for several thousand political positions has overloaded the presidential personnel system. Federal agencies are often left rudderless for 18 months or more as the purely political process of selecting loyal presidential appointees drags on. Indeed, presidential scholar G. Calvin Mackenzie figures that the Bush administration got off the slowest start in at least 30 years. Bush appointees, on average, required 8.1 months to gain confirmation, compared to 5.3 months for Reagan's appointees, and 2.4 months for Kennedy's nominees.[31]

Some of the delay is purely bureaucratic. Government employment forms have acquired a formidable complexity, their completion often requiring applicants to obtain the assistance of attorneys and accountants. Security checks by the Federal Bureau of Investigation have become more complicated and contribute to the backlog.

Ironically, despite the angling for top jobs by the powerful and would-be powerful, it is often very difficult to find truly qualified people to serve in senior slots. Recruiters for the last several presidents have reported that they were forced to approach second-and third-choice candidates before finding willing, and suitable, individuals.

IN THE RANKS

There is a growing concern in the agencies, especially among the Senior Executive Service, that the quality of political appointees at the subcabinet level is deteriorating as superior candidates decline positions and many jobs are filled by less qualified, though loyal, campaign workers and the party faithful.

Positions Filled by Less Qualified Candidates

Motivated less by public service than personal aggrandizement, many of these politically appointed government officials show little devotion to their work or to the agencies they ostensibly manage. And many senior positions rapidly change hands as the politically connected move on to ever more lucrative jobs. Short stints in government may be wonderful résumé builders, but they are poor agency builders. The average tenure of political appointees declined steadily from 2.8 years to 2.0 years by 1984, at the end of Reagan's first term. Between 1964 and 1984, 42 percent of the cabinet secretaries, 62 percent of the deputy secretaries, and 46 percent of undersecretaries left their jobs in 18 months or less. Between 1979 and 1986, some 40 percent of political appointees governmentwide stayed in their jobs less than one year.[32]

It is not surprising, furthermore, that some of the government's most persistently troubled programs have had rapid turnover in their management positions. For instance, the Federal Housing Administration, a division of the Department of Housing and Urban Development, which has lost billions of dollars in recent years through fraud, waste, and abuse, has gone through 12 assistant secretaries of housing in 12 years. Likewise, NASA's space station program, now late and over-budget, has had five managers in seven years.

Even when political appointees are sitting behind their desks, there is some concern that leaving their agency a better operation is not among their chief ambitions. Senior career managers, for instance, discount many of the political appointees' management skills and their grasp of agency programs. A U.S. Merit Systems Protection Board survey of former career executives found that just one-quarter believed political executives brought valuable experience to their jobs, and just 27 percent of the former civil servants thought that political appointees use their positions to make long-term improvements to the management of government.[33] Conversely, 83 percent of political appointees expressed the opinion that career executives bring valuable experience to their jobs, and 60 percent said that career executives view their jobs as an opportunity to improve government service.[34]

Tension Mounts throughout Government

This tension manifests itself throughout government, in the attitudes of senior managers to their political supervisors, in the reasons they leave federal service, and in the management style established by many agency executives. Such cabinet members as James A. Baker III, secretary of state, and Jack Kemp, secretary of housing and urban development, have little interaction with senior managers and, presumably, obtain little of the experienced advice they can offer. Indeed, about 63 percent of former SES managers said that the politicization of their agency was at least partly responsible for their decision to leave the government.[35]

Surveys Show Power Loss over Public Policy

A recent study by two political scientists, Joel D. Aberbach and Bert A. Rockman, confirms existing perceptions that senior career executives have lost influence and power over public policy. A similar survey of top civil servants taken in 1970 revealed that career public servants saw little difference between their influence over policy and the influence of agency heads. By 1986, however, 16 years later, this group's perception of its influence had dropped by nearly a factor of three. Career executives in the latter study had less influence than any other group that had a role in policy formulation, including interest groups, members of Congress, and agency heads.[36] Conversely, the Aberbach/Rockman study shows that in the same time period there has been a doubling in the percentage of civil servants who believe congressional leaders have a great deal of influence over policy.

During the 16 years between studies, senior civil servants became more isolated from the policy process, reporting that their contacts with virtually all groups, from the White House to the public, had declined. This change occurred while the role of political appointees in maintaining a broad base of contacts throughout the policy establishment remained largely unchanged. Indeed, it is hard not to reach the authors' conclusion: "All in all . . . efforts by the Reagan White House to decrease the policy role of civil servants were remarkably successful."[37]

Political Appointments Should Be Reduced for a Better Government

Most studies on political-career relationships have in recent years recommended that the number of political appointments be reduced in the federal government. The Volcker Commission, the National Academy of Public Administration, and the General Accounting Office have suggested that the growth in political appointments may be excessive. Such observers now contend that the damage done to agency effectiveness, to public service morale, and to nonpartisan program administration has offset the advantages gained by political appointees' ideas and the presidential mandates they're supposed to help implement. Stricter limitations on the number of political appointees have been suggested by public service organizations, federal unions, and other groups, but Congress has not shown much interest. After all, powerful legislators regularly promote their own candidates for executive branch positions. If successfully appointed, such individuals presumably show more sensitivity to their patrons' interests than would a career official owing no political allegiance. Mainly for reasons of politics and personal gain, therefore, this harmful practice, creeping politicization, will continue unabated.

Chapter Five

The Management Mess

T he number of passengers boarding at U.S. airports increased from 278 million in 1978 to 482 million in 1988. By the year 2000, the number is expected to top 750 million, but the Federal Aviation Administration's (FAA) air traffic control system only operates as long as the nation's supply of the 1950's era vacuum tubes last.

The number of illegal aliens crossing the nation's porous southern border continues to rise, and in recent years has topped 1 million, estimates the Immigration and Naturalization Service. However, many of the surveillance aircraft flown by the U.S. Border Patrol are in such disrepair that they no longer can be safely operated.

Account information is so unreliable at the Farmers Home Administration (FHA), which provides credit for agriculture and rural development, that the agency's financial control systems were unable to project losses on its $22 billion direct farm loan portfolio because information was either unavailable or inaccurate.

MISMANAGEMENT PROBLEMS OF THE GOVERNMENT

The federal government is falling apart. Not only can the government not manage the programs and services it provides to Americans, it cannot even manage itself. The equipment and systems, the buildings and business practices, needed to effectively operate a $1.54 trillion enterprise, are woefully neglected—where they exist at all. Federal management systems, by and large, have not kept pace with the demands this nation

places on its national government. In an age of advanced computers and sophisticated information systems, federal agencies
are still in the era of vacuum tubes, handwritten ledgers, and,
until the end of the 1980s at the Federal Communications Commission, rotary dial telephones. Accounting and other basic
management systems cannot produce the data needed for intelligent analysis and planning. Massive federal structures
such as the Pentagon are literally falling apart.

Politicians in the Federal Infrastructure

Blame the politicians first for the lack of investment in federal
infrastructure, for poor design and maintenance of modern facilities, and then for the failure to procure modern computers.
Though inexcusable, the reason for inadequate attention to
management is readily apparent: Few politicians consider investment in the government to be very important. In large
part, then, hollow government exists because lawmakers are
rarely willing to focus their time and energy on the agencies'
underlying problems.

No member of Congress can expect to stay in office by looking after the management of government. Jobs and services for
their constituents are what count to lawmakers, not, for the
most part, the viability of the FAA's computers or fixing the
FHA's accounting shortcomings. Though Congress pursues a
range of oversight activities, few are a serious or sustained attempt to improve federal management. Rather, they tend to be
brief bursts of activity in hopes of gaining a hometown newspaper headline or a 30-second television sound bite. After all,
program creation, not maintenance, has always been the headline grabber.

Simply put, most legislators see little advantage in investing
scarce time and energy, to say nothing of federal dollars, into
programs that won't immediately benefit their constituency.
As a result, long-term investment in equipment, maintenance,
training, and management support goes unfunded or, at best,
neglected. Repairs to buildings are ignored; training and new
computer systems are deferred.

Members of Executive Branch Ignore Responsibilities

Members of the president's cabinet take office determined to have an impact on the day's most important public policy issues. In the few years before the next election, most pursue the broad policy goals upon which the president, who just hired them, was elected, and hopes to be reelected. Few, if any, concern themselves with the day-to-day management requirements needed to keep the government working well.

Moreover, on the rare occasion that a political appointee recognizes the importance of investing in the government's management and infrastructure, the pressures of policymaking and the short tenure typical of most noncareer federal executives hampers that individual's efforts to improve an agency's operations and organizations.

Politicians, whether in the White House or on Capitol Hill, endeavor to spend the government's limited funds on those programs that were the pillars of their campaigns. What's more, in their rush to put in place the programs promised during their campaigns, politicians give little attention to the resources needed to effectively implement them beyond the short term. As a result, the agencies charged with administering the promised programs too often get little or no additional budget authority or personnel. Thus, agencies must ignore other important duties or provide fewer resources to an ever growing list of responsibilities. Tight budgets at many agencies mean that when new high-profile programs get added to their duties, they often have little choice but to cut back the provision of other services.

Government's Inability to Manage Its Affairs

Perhaps the most fundamental flaw of the federal government is its seemingly perpetual inability to manage its affairs. The problems that most Americans have with Washington (i.e., the waste, fraud and abuse, the propensity to ignore clear warnings, or not to learn from mistakes) all are the result of inadequate or nonexistent management systems.

- How, otherwise, to explain that the crimes and abuses at the Department of Housing and Urban Development (HUD) in the 1980s were virtually no different from the crimes and abuses at the department in the 1950s?[1]
- What else accounts for the many reports, the dozens of repetitive recommendations, urging overhaul of the Pentagon's procurement system in the past 30 years? In the early 1980s, the Department of Defense was embarrassed for paying $435 for a hammer and $640 for a toilet cover. The Pentagon recently paid $1,868 for a toilet cover for a C-5 transport aircraft—and seemingly has learned nothing from the past.[2]
- NASA's management system for detecting major safety flaws in the space shuttle, supposedly strengthened in the aftermath of the 1986 *Challenger* accident, did not prevent five shuttle flights from taking off with faulty sensors in 1990 and 1991.[3]

The problems of the government seem never to get fixed. Try as they might, and government officials do try, efforts at reform seldom work. The reforms are either ignored or prove so cumbersome that the "improvements" often are worse than the original problems. Recent federal procurement reform laws drive up prices and delay purchases; ethics regulations now discourage open communications between government program managers and contractors and discourage talented people from joining the government.

Cuts in Public Funds Share the Blame

Much of the mismanagement stems from the government's miserable record of strategic planning, program evaluation, and management reviews. Though periodic attempts to link planning and budgets have occurred in government, most such efforts have been abandoned. Likewise, severe cuts in program evaluation units during the 1980s have left the government with little capability to determine how its programs are working, and whether or not the agencies spend public funds effectively. A General Accounting Office (GAO) study found that program analysis staffs throughout the government decreased by 22 percent between 1980 and 1984. A follow-up study of 15 evaluation offices showed an additional 12 percent drop by 1988.[4]

Similarly, funds for agency program evaluations decreased by 37 percent between 1980 and 1984, and another 6 percent between 1984 and 1988. In 1988, the GAO said, "Throughout many federal agencies, the information pipeline for program oversight and management is drying up. . . . Basic data are lacking on wide-ranging issues such as health care quality, the state of the environment, and the results of weapons testing."[5]

This weakness in planning, evaluation, and review has had serious consequences throughout government:

- The Bureau of Land Management, an Interior Department agency that is steward to 272 million acres of public land, has lost more than $90 million in revenues since 1986 simply through poor management on its forest lands in western Oregon.[6]

- The Department of Veterans Affairs has hired physicians at its medical centers without first checking their backgrounds or verifying their medical licenses. Less than one-half of the physicians hired between 1986 and 1988 had gone through VA's credentialing procedure that requires the department to obtain licensing information from state medical boards.[7]

- An investigation of overcharges and mismanagement of the Pentagon's B-2 Stealth Bomber program by the Justice Department found that the Air Force had been fully aware for years that the contractor was providing inaccurate information about costs and schedules, knew about cost overruns and delays—and had taken "no remedial action."[8] Similarly, in 1991, the Navy continued to give a division of Northrop Corp. Pentagon contracts after it pleaded guilty to falsifying test results on weapons components and was supposedly barred from government work.[9]

- For more than a decade, government and private contract managers at the Hanford, Washington, federal nuclear reservation have known (but did not let superiors know) that there has been a buildup of combustible gases in storage tanks containing 64 million gallons of highly radioactive liquid waste. Serious health and environmental damage could result if the gases exploded.

THE ACCOUNTING AGONY

The government's finances are a mess. Today, agencies of the largest, most expensive government in the world often have no control over the billions of dollars in public funds they manage. Accounting systems are woefully inadequate and antiquated, inventory and other data systems often are unautomated, and a multitude of disparate procedures frustrate any attempts to unify the government's budget, accounting, program, and financial management activities.

The Treasury Act of 1789

To be sure, it didn't start out that way. The Treasury Act of 1789 set up the basic elements of financial management when it established the positions of comptroller and auditor in Alexander Hamilton's fledgling Department of the Treasury. In the nation's early years, the need for revenue collection and debt payment was so important that by 1801, the Treasury Department employed more than one-half of the government's civilian workers.[10] Unlike the early State and War Departments, the Treasury Department for years virtually reported to Congress, since it was the legislature, not the president, that was responsible for federal finances.

The Office of Management and Budget

Nevertheless, the government for most of its existence has had no formal and comprehensive budgeting and accounting procedures. It took more than a century, until the Dockery Act of 1894, for the comptroller to gain complete control over the government's auditing and accounting functions. And it was not until after World War I, with passage of the Budget and Accounting Act of 1921, that a centralized budget and review of agency appropriations requests were established. This same law also created the twin pillars of today's federal financial structure: The General Accounting Office with its comptroller general, and the Bureau of the Budget, originally within the Treasury Department. The budget bureau was shifted in 1939 to the executive office of the president and later reorganized and strengthened into the now uniquely powerful Office of Management and Budget (OMB).

The primary purpose of the 1921 law was to centralize and strengthen the government's budgeting and accounting procedures—they had proved inadequate to the demands of World War I. But the unprecedented expansion and expenditures of the government during the New Deal and World War II essentially thwarted consolidation efforts. So complicated and diffuse had the government's accounting practices become by the end of World War II that Congress recognized the obvious and simply institutionalized the decentralized system that had informally emerged. As part of the Budget and Accounting Procedures Act of 1950, Congress gave agency heads responsibility for accounting and financial management systems.

Agency Heads' Lack of Responsibility

The results largely have been devastating. With little coordination or emphasis on financial management, the government has seen a proliferation of hundreds of accounting systems, payroll systems, inventory procedures, and financial standards. An inability or unwillingness to focus on internal controls, in a period of unprecedented growth in the government's credit programs and other financial commitments, has led to unchecked waste, fraud, and abuse. And when it comes to administering federal services, most agencies are simply unable to determine how much money they have spent or received. Even fewer can decide whether those funds were used effectively.

Vast discrepancies occur each year between the figures compiled by agencies and the numbers turned up by GAO or other auditors. One example: The Department of Labor's fiscal 1988 financial reports to the Treasury Department listed $2 billion in liabilities, yet an audited financial statement by the department's inspector general calculated liabilities of $25 billion.

In no better condition is the Farmers Home Administration, whose large portfolio of acquired property in many cases cannot be verified or valued, and where future farm loan losses often cannot be projected.

Similarly, the Federal Housing Administration's financial report for fiscal 1988 identified losses of $858 million, but the GAO tallied red ink of $4.2 billion. In a recent letter to Congress, the GAO advised that losses for fiscal 1989, the most recent year for which figures are available, would exceed the previous year's by more than 50 percent, and that losses should be expected for the next several years.[11]

Breakdown of Government Bookkeeping

These examples constitute just a portion of the enormous losses—and even greater potential for losses—evident in the manifest breakdown of the government's bookkeeping. And these losses are, in turn, just a fraction of the government's total $6.2 trillion in possible liabilities tied to federal credit and insurance programs. So worried is OMB about the apparent lack of internal controls at federal agencies after the scandals at HUD, and the potential for waste, fraud, and abuse inherent in such weaknesses, that the small agency has begun to seek out the worst cases in the hopes of stemming further losses.

Indeed, a list of more than 100 of the most worrisome cases now appears in the government's annual budget document, in part to keep pressure on agencies to improve. Still, OMB officials acknowledge that even this rogue's roster is but a sample of how truly messed-up the government's financial systems are. Some of the problems include:

- The U.S. Customs Service, which received $19 billion in 1990 import duty, is second only to the Internal Revenue Service in collecting revenues. Yet Customs can't verify how much it takes in, suggesting the possibility of fraud and abuse at the agency. Customs' Asset Forfeiture Fund, which manages and disposes of billions of dollars of repossessed properties from drug felons, has a weak control over assets and inventory sales.[12]

- Food stamp fraud in the Agriculture Department's Food and Nutrition Service costs the government more than $100 million annually. The agency's inability to match the number of coupons issued with their redemption by banks costs another $200 million each year.[13]
- The Urban Mass Transportation Administration, responsible for parceling out $3 billion each year in grants to local transit authorities, has not made sure that grantees use of $30 billion in outstanding funds complies with federal regulations. Such weak internal controls mean that untold billions could be misused.[14]
- The Bureau of Indian Affairs, which manages many Indian reservations' health, education, and cultural programs, was unable to account for $95 million (some 10 percent of appropriations) in its fiscal 1990 budget. Investigators found sloppy accounting practices and weak computer security. Almost the entire staff of the bureau could access and alter computerized accounting records. Even people who were not federal employees had access to computers storing the agency's accounts.[15]

Government's Inability to Rectify Financial Woes

Unfortunately, the agencies' efforts to fix their financial fiascos have met with marginal success. Accounting systems, when they are at all automated, are often antiquated and in disrepair. Although the government spends hundreds of millions of dollars on attempts to improve its systems, they are uncoordinated, leaving them unable to produce timely and accurate information. Design flaws, inexperience in assessing requirements for accounting systems, and poor program management have doomed attempts by many agencies to overhaul their computers. During the 1980s, for instance, the Navy was forced to scrap a new, but totally inadequate, automated management information system after spending an estimated $230 million over nine years.[16]

What's more, it is not infrequent for government agencies to run huge, multibillion dollar operations and programs without modern computer systems. Most records for HUD's scandal-ridden Section 8 housing program are still handled manually;

benefit and insurance programs run by the Department of Veterans Affairs use 1960s batch-style computer card technology; and the U.S. Air Force tallies much of its inventory by sight.

Agencies, because of disparate accounting systems and standards, often can't make sense of the data they do have. Not only is much of the information outdated, but there is often no way to reconcile information from the same program that comes out of separate field offices and regions. Thus, cabinet secretaries seeking to shift funds from one program to another in the middle of the year, for instance, typically cannot obtain reliable information about how much money remains unspent in any given program.

Executive Branch Attempts to Improve Financial Systems

The executive branch has taken steps to improve the desultory performance of its financial systems. The Carter administration began the first serious effort to modernize and integrate the hundreds of disparate federal accounting systems, a program that Ronald Reagan's OMB revamped and strengthened under Reform 88. Moreover, the legacy of the HUD scandal has prompted closer attention to reports on internal controls issued by agencies in conformance with the 1982 Federal Managers' Financial Integrity Act. Additional resources have been funneled to financial management projects and to agencies' inspectors general. The Bush administration, for instance, had sought to increase funding for financial management to $1.8 billion in fiscal 1992, a 338 percent rise over fiscal 1991.[17] But Congress approved just a fraction of those funds.

Legislative remedies, including the Inspector General Act of 1978 and the Federal Managers' Financial Integrity Act of 1982, were designed to help agencies bolster internal controls and stem abusive and illegal financial practices. Yet, agencies do not always adequately follow these laws. Further, a 1990 law creates for most executive branch departments a position of chief financial officer, which, if permitted to wield the power provided by the law, should help agencies better consolidate and upgrade their accounting systems and improve internal controls.

Nonetheless, the breakdown in the agencies' internal controls (where they exist at all) will prove stubbornly hard to fix. Problems with financial integrity, of course, were behind much of the housing program losses at the Department of Housing and Urban Development. For instance, soon after his arrival at HUD, Secretary Jack Kemp said that some 40 internal control weaknesses had been found in a review of the scandal, and that actions would be taken to correct them. Many remain uncorrected today.

Throughout most of the 1980s, in fact, HUD's managers were well aware of critical financial management problems but generally refused to face them. Indeed, as losses from fraud and mismanagement mounted in 1987, HUD officials even falsely certified to Congress and to the president that certain serious weaknesses with the department's financial management did not exist, and that a review of accounting systems in the previous year revealed no major problems. To reach such a conclusion was to literally ignore a raft of reports prepared by both the department's inspector general and private sector accounting firms that warned about ineffective accounting and management systems. Throughout the government, just as in the private sector, management attention makes a difference. As a 1990 Senate investigation concluded: "This crucial responsibility was itself abused and not taken seriously by HUD's top management."[18]

FEDERAL FACILITIES

Parts of the federal government have become so hollow (quite literally) that they are falling down. More than 200 historic buildings owned by the government at the Virgin Islands National Park are crumbling under years of neglect and disrepair.

Repair and investment have increasingly given way to austerity and inattention, as depicted:

- National Park Service and Forest Service roads are often so washed out and full of holes as to defy safe driving.
- Federal office buildings across the country, from Washington, D.C. to San Francisco, Calif., are in poor condition, and often unsafe themselves. Some of the most

venerable buildings in the capital, the Pentagon, the
Lincoln and Jefferson Memorials, the Agriculture and
Interior Departments, have sadly deteriorated and will
require billions of dollars in repair and additional
maintenance.

- Even the U.S. Capitol needs help. In 1990 it sprung a
leak from its famous dome, dripping water from its fres-
cos to the marbled floor below.

Condition of Washington's Public Buildings

Washington has not invested in itself. The buildings of the federal government are commonly crowded, poorly maintained,
and inadequately ventilated. Tools such as computers, trucks,
and laboratory equipment often are antiquated, insufficient,
and sometimes simply unavailable. The neglect of the government's facilities and equipment not only hinders federal employees from effectively providing public services, but its sad
shape discourages people from working for Washington in the
first place. Indeed, a survey of federal personnel specialists in
16 cities found that nearly one-third of them believed that poor
working conditions have a detrimental impact on government's ability to recruit and retain employees.[19]

The government's marble buildings and memorials are
grand and imposing. Yet they also need more than $4 billion in
repairs and renovations that have been deferred, in some instances, for more than a decade.[20]

The Failure of the General Services Administration

Since the federal government is a vast enterprise, so too are its
real estate requirements. The General Services Administration
(GSA), landlord and facilities manager to Uncle Sam, manages
and oversees 245 million square feet of space in 6,600 buildings. And unlike the private sector, where buildings often exchange hands, many of Washington's best-known facilities will
remain in the government's care for the foreseeable future.
Thus, repairs and renovations, as well as provisions to protect
employees' safety and health, when deferred simply create

larger, more expensive problems later. Not only have many federal buildings been neglected, to the point where major repairs and alterations are needed, but the deterioration will undoubtedly worsen because more than one-half of the government's buildings are already at least 40 years old.

The upkeep required for such extensive property holdings is neither easy nor inexpensive, but funding limitations and ineffective management have compounded these problems. The GSA spent about $709 million in fiscal 1991 to repair federal facilities, some $148 million less than was spent in fiscal 1990. No surprise, then, that the GAO concluded in a recent study of federal facilities that the Federal Buildings Fund has not produced the revenue required to finance many of the needed repairs and alterations. Moreover, GAO reported that the General Services Administration lacks much of the data needed to manage buildings and has not developed a system for responding to the increasing maintenance requirements of its aging facilities.[21]

Safety and Health Hazards Ignored

Of special concern is that safety and health hazards in many of the government's office buildings have been ignored. Secure parking lots, fire alarms, and sprinkler systems, even proper ventilation are simply unavailable at many government sites. Building temperatures at the Federal Aviation Administration's headquarters range from 55 degrees to 95 degrees on any given day; workers are sent home on days when the building can't be properly cooled.

Not surprisingly, such inferior working conditions take their toll on productivity and morale in the civil service. Most federal employees recognize that public funds ought not be spent on plush offices, but at the same time, adequate quarters signal not only a professional atmosphere but a respect for public service.

Deficiencies in Federal Buildings

Many of the deficiencies in federal buildings would surely not be tolerated in the private sector:

- An elevator at the Federal Aviation Administration broke
  down so frequently that even the agency's administrator
  was trapped. Frequent power overloads and outages at
  the FAA's headquarters have at times prevented the
  agency's employees from using computerized flight
  information.[22]
- Investment in the 50-year-old Pentagon has been so ignored that more than $1 billion must be spent to repair
  and renovate a decade's worth of accumulated neglect.
  Until 1988, the building's original coal boilers heated the
  Pentagon and its heating, air conditioning, and electrical
  systems were so unreliable that they threatened national
  security. The General Services Administration so mismanaged the building, in fact, that Congress in 1990
  turned the Pentagon's maintenance over to the Department of Defense.
- Conditions are so bad at the 52-story-building where the
  National Aeronautics and Space Administration builds
  the space shuttle that concrete falls from the roof; NASA
  has been forced to string netting across the ceiling above
  the shuttle to catch falling debris.[23] It is so damp and
  musty in some Marshall Space Flight Center offices that
  small mushrooms and moss have sprouted on the win-
  dow sills.

The General Services Administration's lack of funds and a
tendency to put off major repairs has resulted in an overall deterioration that could have been avoided. For instance, an aged
10-inch water pipe broke in 1990 and flooded 350,000 square
feet of the Pentagon's basement heating plant, the primary
electrical switching room, and the Air Force's Communications
Center. Besides disrupting electrical power and interfering
with Air Force operations, the burst pipe cost an estimated
$500,000 in property damage.[24]

Government's Investment in Equipment No Better

The government's investment in equipment is generally no
better than its investment in buildings. Federal laboratories
and research centers, once renowned for their expertise and

state-of-the-art facilities, are now often second rate compared to private industry and academic institutions. Research equipment has aged and been neglected at the Centers for Disease Control, the Food and Drug Administration, the Environmental Protection Agency, and even the military's labs. The EPA's work in air pollution standards is hampered by inferior equipment and at the FDA, "much of their scientific equipment is obsolete and technologically inadequate," a recent report concludes.[25] Laboratory equipment at one FDA unit, the Center for Devices and Radiological Health, has been called "antiquated" by the American Society for Microbiology.[26]

Office equipment is in no better shape. Shortages of photocopy paper, and the lack of money for more of it, at the Social Security Administration has forced employees to purchase their own supplies. Professional staff at the Consumer Product Safety Commission at times have had to buy their own computer programs and fix antiquated equipment because the agency couldn't afford to pick up the tab.

Other equipment also has deteriorated. New National Park Service vehicles are a rare find in the field. Some parks have just one or two vehicles (typically old and with holes in the floorboards) to handle vast terrains. The staff at the Death Valley National Monument, with 2 million acres of desert to oversee, through much of the 1980s had one aging pickup truck in which to make the rounds. Indeed, National Park Service Director James M. Ridenour was shocked over the disrepair of the parks when he took office: "I saw working conditions that were really unacceptable: People didn't have the tools; they didn't have the equipment that they should have."[27] Sometimes there is not even an office. For years the Congaree Swamp National Monument has been administered out of an office 25 miles distant, in Columbia, South Carolina.

COMPUTERS CANNOT COMPUTE

At the Los Angeles International Airport in February 1991, a USAir 737 jetliner and a small commuter plane collided on a busy runway, killing 34 people. At fault was an air traffic

controller, who federal investigators say allowed the smaller
plane onto the runway to await takeoff clearance, then let the
737 land on the same runway.

Also at fault were the air traffic control computers. The 20-
year-old vacuum tube-powered ground radar, which would
have allowed the controller to see the commuter plane on the
runway, had been inoperative for two days before the crash.
Although repairs had been ordered, none had been made by
the time of the collision.

Computer Problems among the Agencies

The FAA is one of many federal agencies that suffer from long-
festering computer problems whose primary cause is disinvestment. Agencies throughout the government are tackling
increasing work loads in data processing and other tasks on 15-
year-old, sometimes 20-year-old computers. The Defense Nuclear Agency until the 1990s chugged along with a 22-year-old
mainframe. And the U.S. government is the Western world's
largest buyer of vacuum tubes, the grandfathers of today's
microprocessors, in part for the FAA's ground radars.

Being behind the times diminishes the quality of services
government is supposed to provide its citizens. The VA is a
case in point: Managers do not have information readily available to assess the quality of health care or the effectiveness of
the services provided to veterans. Information is contained in
more than 150 fragmented automated systems and many informally developed manual systems. The information is not efficiently collected, it often must be manually transcribed and can
take up to two months to reach the desks of agency top managers. Further, information is duplicated through the systems,
and is often incomplete and inaccurate. Such "weaknesses
have hindered VA's ability to effectively manage programs and
have contributed to service delays," concluded a report of the
General Accounting Office.[28]

The IRS is in even worse shape. Computers at the government's largest collection agency are 30 years old; their sequen-
tial batch processing format means not only tremendous delays
while computer tape is shipped to a central computer site, but

that lost or damaged tapes equal lost or damaged tax returns. The former IRS Commissioner Lawrence Gibbs says, "The government once was a leader in computers. . . . Today, the IRS's computer system is somewhere in the ice age. It's inefficient, and it wasn't made to handle the amount of work that's being demanded of it."[29]

Crucial Problems with Computer Equipment and Services

The government does spend increasing amounts on computer equipment and services; about $20 billion in fiscal 1991, compared to $9 billion in 1982. But this growth masks a crucial problem: As with other capital equipment budgets, much of the money is spent for new automation projects, which leaves less for upgrading and maintaining the vast computer kingdom that the government has amassed in the past 25 years.

Even when funds are earmarked for replacing old computers, the task of getting the system up and operating is often woefully managed. The IRS is now undertaking its third try in 15 years to modernize its computers after the first two attempts failed. The FAA has spent more than a decade designing the National Airspace System Plan, a high-tech upgrade for the outmoded computers, like the one at the Los Angeles Airport, that currently control the nation's air traffic. The plan's complexity is part of the problem, but so too is the agency's troubles in retaining a staff talented enough to design and install the proper system.

Former FAA chiefs also have complained that high turnover in the agency's legal and procurement staffs has delayed the acquisition of the system, the most expensive domestic computer procurement project since NASA geared up for the Apollo program. These problems, combined with the intractable rules and red tape associated with most federal procurements, have put the FAA's air traffic control modernization hopelessly behind schedule. A 1981 plan was expected to take 10 years and $11 billion to complete improvements; the system now won't be finished before the year 2000 and is likely to cost more than $30 billion.

Unfortunately, the FAA is not alone. Many of the biggest, most complex federal computer procurements designed to replace aging, overworked systems, are years late, understaffed, and significantly over budget. Every one of these agencies has at the same time experienced tremendous growth in their work loads, thus increasing the demand for efficient, modern computer systems. The Social Security Administration, the Internal Revenue Service, the Health Care Financing Administration, the National Weather Service, the Patent and Trademark Office, are among the agencies facing uncertain futures in which the ability to fulfill their mission may be compromised by failing computers that can wait no longer for replacements.

The Department of Justice, for instance, may have a hard time managing the $2.7 billion worth of data processing hardware and software it plans to buy between 1991 and 1995. It claims to have neither the staff adequate to supervise the acquisitions nor managers capable of seeing that the systems are properly used.[30]

A $3 billion upgrade of the National Weather Service computers is so far behind schedule that its dependence on aging 1950s-era equipment could hamper its ability to warn the public of dangerous storms. Consider the flood killing 26 people in Shadyside, Ohio, in the summer of 1990: the weather service radar near Akron, Ohio, was too weak to determine the extent of the storm and so did not issue warnings of imminent danger. Unfortunately, staff cuts at the Akron office—part of agencywide reductions made by overeager budgeteers before the new system designed to take their place was ready—left meteorologists unable to gather sufficient information about the storm in adequate time to warn the public.[31]

Radars originally scheduled to be installed starting in 1990 now are not expected to be ready until 1997, and the next-generation satellites designed to replace the weather service's one remaining dying orbiter are so defective that they probably won't be launched in time. As a result, the nation faces the possibility of having no satellite weather assessments after 1992, when the remaining satellite is expected to stop functioning. Recent agency assessments of the modernization plan found that every phase of the program has been delayed by management errors and design flaws. "By traditional measures of successful systems development, the agency has serious problems," Inspector General Francis D. DeGeorge of the Commerce Department wrote in a 1990 report to Congress. "Costs are increasing, technical performance standards are not being met and the schedule is seriously slipping."[32]

And so it is with the government overall. Whether buildings or computers, accounting systems or internal controls, Washington's ability to manage the world's single largest organization has a long way to go before it is modern and efficient.

Chapter Six

Shadow Government

A dmiral James Watkins seemed comfortable enough in the glare of the hearing room's bright lights as he explained his intention to spend $155 billion to mop up toxic and radioactive waste at U.S. nuclear weapons production plants. "I have already begun to develop solutions to these problems," the secretary of energy told the House Armed Services Committee's panel on the Department of Energy nuclear facilities. "DOE is developing timetables and schedules that demonstrate that we have a plan and milestones from which progress and success can be measured over a realistic period."[1]

Aides to Watkins nodded approvingly from the audience that day in early April of 1989, and panel members praised the well-regarded former chief of naval operations for getting the Energy Department back on track after decades of safety and environmental problems.

Some time later, however, the panel was less pleased to discover that neither Watkins nor anyone else in his department had written the testimony the panel had heard. Instead, it had been crafted in large part by BDM International Inc., a Department of Energy and Defense Department consultant, as part of a subcontract to provide support services.[2]

This is not the government most Americans think of when paying taxes or visiting Washington, D.C. But more and more it is the government that Americans get.

GROWTH OF AN UNFETTERED GOVERNMENT

As the federal work load has expanded through three decades of added mandates ranging from entitlements to environmental protection to space exploration, the work force has not grown comparatively. Fears of unfettered government growth, along with a hulking budget deficit, have constrained the size of America's national bureaucracy. Between 1960 and 1992, federal outlays increased from $340.4 billion to $1 trillion in constant (1982) dollars. Yet the government's civilian employment has remained remarkably constant during these same 32 years. What's more, when measured against the growth of the nation's population, the federal establishment has actually been shrinking ever since its 1968 peak of 14.7 employees for every 1,000 citizens.[3] Though government employment of all types has more than doubled in the past 30 years, most of the increase has been at the state and local levels. Twenty-eight percent of the country's civil servants were in the federal bureaucracy in 1960, compared to just 17 percent today.[4] Indeed, the federal payroll declined from 25 percent of the federal budget in 1971 to about 17 percent by 1991 as total employment— including all three federal branches and the Postal Service— slipped from 5.6 million to 5.2 million.[5]

Demands on Government Rise; Resources Inactive

The demands on government rise while its resources stagnate. Not surprisingly, this dichotomy has had unpleasant consequences for the government and its programs. Truth is, what we often think of as Washington today is not the government at all. Vital federal functions are not always performed by public-minded civil servants, but often by private corporations engaging in public activities to earn profits. The result is "Shadow Government," in which people other than civil servants carry out ostensibly federal activities.[6] The cost is considerable: Accountability and public expertise are lost; conflicts of interest, questions of fairness, and other problems are raised.

Significantly, federal contractors are only part of the issue. Little noticed is the fundamental shift in the past few decades of not just *who* delivers government services to Americans, but also *how* such services are delivered. The steady growth of social programs, the advancement of regulatory and economic agendas, have in large measure been accomplished through a remarkable change in the forms of federal action. More than ever before, the government is less the producer than the provider of services to its citizens. Government more and more is turning to relatively new tools, including grants and subsidies, loans, guarantees, and insurance, to try to meet policy objectives. The actual implementation of many government programs has been handed off to private companies, to nonprofit organizations, and to agencies of state and local governments.

PRIVATE INVESTMENTS

Since the time of Thomas Jefferson, many politicians and the people electing them frequently have felt that public sector investments were private sector disinvestments. They have believed that resources, whether capital, natural, or human, could be most productive when employed in the private sector to advance the nation's wealth.

Americans' distrust of their government has complemented this notion. We always have wanted Washington to have no more power, people, or permanence than was absolutely essential. Our distaste for bureaucracy, our historic distrust of authority, compels us to guard against government's growth. Ronald Reagan's determination during the 1980s to privatize government activities—from export financing to weather forecasting—was a dramatic and recent manifestation of this suspicion. Reagan and like-minded conservatives throughout the country considered that each sale of federal assets to the private sector, every government service contracted out, helped loosen government's growing hold over its citizens, with the added benefit of lower taxpayer costs. If only it were this simple!

Federal Fiscal Problems Expand Shadow Government

In recent years, federal fiscal troubles have enlarged the Shadow Government. The spending constraints imposed by Gramm-Rudman, the impact of budget cuts, and the seemingly uncontrollable federal budget deficit itself—all have sent administrations and executive agencies scrambling for ways to do more with fewer resources. Indeed, both Republican and Democratic presidents have become adept at political sleights of hand: They have provided programs demanded by voters while holding federal employment steady so that no one might accuse them of making big government bigger.

Shadow Government is the sorcery that allows administrations to manage this feat. Indeed, Ronald Reagan, who conservatives still champion for shrinking the size of the government, really did nothing of the sort. He merely shifted the government from the sunlight to the shadows. For instance, though the Reagan administration cut the bureaucracy at the Energy Department, it also quietly tripled the department's budget for consultants. In fact, domestic agencies throughout the federal government lost much of their staff in the 1980s, only to find that civil servants were being replaced by higher cost private consultants. In many cases, the government's work was simply shifted from the public to the private sector, where salaries were higher and the national interest took a backseat to profits.

FEDERAL CONTRACTORS

Inherently, there is nothing wrong with the private sector providing public goods. The government has always used contractors to obtain or deliver needed services. The Continental Army at Valley Forge contracted out to local farmers and merchants for the food and shelter it needed to survive the harsh Pennsylvania winter of 1777. Even then, however, some contractors ripped off the government, providing shoddy goods, and sometimes nothing at all, for the funds they received. In the 19th century, mail was distributed by private entrepreneurs. The famous Pinkerton detective organization got its start as a spy contractor for the Union during the Civil War.

To be sure, the government could not fulfill its public responsibilities without the work of private contractors. Since the government produces few goods itself, it must rely on contractors for what it consumes. The government's consumption is huge: It spent some $178 billion in fiscal 1990 for everything from toilet paper to Tomahawk missiles.[7] Roughly three-quarters of what the government contracts for is to sustain the military, primarily in the research, development, and production of Pentagon weapon systems.[8]

The greatest growth in federal contracting has occurred since World War II, as the Cold War and its arms race demanded permanent armed forces and produced a never-ending effort to perfect conventional and nuclear weaponry. Washington's regulation of atomic energy, first through the Atomic Energy Commission and later the Department of Energy (DOE), has also drawn many contractors. DOE's 19 research laboratories and production facilities, part of 1,100 federal facilities devoted to the advancement of nuclear weapons, are primarily operated by private firms under government contract.

At the same time, the government helped such federally funded research and development organizations as Mitre Corp. and Rand Corp. to set up shop. The rationale, then as now, was that short-term projects could be accomplished less expensively by a private sector that didn't have to contend with the expense of hiring and training permanent federal workers. Consultants, especially those involved in social sciences, got another federal boost in the rush to implement the Great Society programs of the 1960s. In the 1970s, the government's demand for private expertise grew as a result of a regulatory binge that, ironically, included protecting workers and the environment from harmful practices in the private sector.

Today, the Shadow Government's work force is huge—though documenting its numbers isn't easy. Precise records are not kept by most federal agencies. The most expansive view would include everyone paid through federal contracts. This group, estimated at 3 million by a 1989 National Research Council study, is larger than the government's civilian work force.[9]

There is little conflict about the government's contracting out its massive weapons production or the space shuttle to the private sector; it makes little sense for the government to compete with corporations for such activities. Except for a federal union or two, few are exorcized when the government seeks private contracts for routine maintenance jobs such as garbage collection and lawn mowing at federal facilities, tasks that have little connection to public policy.

Advisory and Assistance Services

Of growing concern, however, has been the more murky world of advisory and assistance services. This is the world of the consultants, the myriad private corporations that in the past two decades have sprouted like weeds in and around Washington. The Cabinet Council on Management and Administration in 1984 figured that the government spends between $4 billion and $20 billion annually on consulting services, but as with private providers of goods to the government, agency records on consultants are often incomplete, or do not differentiate between services provided by contractors and consultants.

What is certain, nevertheless, is that thousands of private companies are now doing much of the work the government has historically done itself. Their activities include preparing agency budgets, writing testimony, interpreting regulations, and evaluating the performance of other private contractors. At certain agencies, the State Department and the Agency for International Development, for instance, thousands of personal service contracts are awarded to specific individuals, many of them former agency officials, with little or no competition.

Also clear is that deficit-driven budget and personnel cuts throughout the 1980s have made agencies more dependent on contractors. In fact, as budgets have tightened, even inspectors general and the General Accounting Office (GAO), long-time critics of Shadow Government, have been hiring private contractors. Inspectors general, for instance, recently have turned to private sector accountants to comb the ledger books of their departments as part of a new law requiring them to audit agency financial statements. Many GAO audits are performed also by private corporations.

Contracting for Services Does Not Save Costs

Though conservatives have long held that contracting out saves money, the opposite often appears to be true, according to the internal audits of the Energy and Defense Departments. The Energy Department pays some 20 percent more to consultants than to federal employees for comparable work. The difference is even more dramatic at the Pentagon, where a wide variety of defense tasks would have been cheaper, in many cases lesser by 50 percent or more, if federal employees had done the work given to the consultants.[10] What's more, though consulting contracts are supposed to be used to secure short-term assistance, contracts examined by the Pentagon's inspector general lasted years, some even decades.[11] Likewise, Energy Department and Environmental Protection Agency (EPA) consultant contracts have been allowed to run for years. In such cases, the consultants are federal employees in all but name. They often sit next to government workers and do similar tasks—all the while making much higher salaries.

Overall, the federal government has been forced into hiring private contractors for two reasons: limitations on the number of employees that Congress and the White House will allow agencies to hire; and a lack of federal expertise within agencies to do the work.[12]

PROBLEMS WITH CONTRACTORS

Private companies' pervasive participation in federal activities raises many important questions about public policy and government operations. They include:

Conflicts of interest. Dozens of companies engaged in contract work for the federal government also do work that conflicts with their public responsibilities. The Defense Department has hired contractors to evaluate the quality and performance of weapons systems that other divisions of the same companies helped to develop. Contractors cleaning up Superfund waste sites for the Environmental Protection Agency have at the same time been advising the companies that dumped the contaminants in the first place. Energy Department contractors investigating contamination at nuclear weapons plants also were employed by the EPA to monitor DOE's compliance with cleanup regulations.

A review of Energy Department procurement operations found that, despite explicit rules, little attention is paid to checking on potential conflicts of interests; there is "significant danger" that a contractor could end up analyzing its own, or a former client's, work.[13]

Accountability.   Consultants increasingly prepare congressional testimony, agency budgets, draft regulations, and program guidelines, work that is clearly the province of federal employees. In the Admiral Watkins episode, private sector contractors not only prepared his testimony but also set up much of the timetable for the more than $150 billion cleanup of hazardous waste at the nation's nuclear weapons production sites.

Critics of contracting are rightfully concerned about the difficulty of determining who is responsible for program administration. Thus, accountability is often disguised, leaving executive officials blameless. Equally difficult is discovering who actually originated public policy—a federal official or a private company? In the case of Watkins's testimony, for example, BDM International Inc., a major consultant to the Energy and Defense Departments, clearly prepared public policy.

Making decisions.   Private consultants have become so important to the agencies for which they work that some wind up making public policy decisions. One example is GEO/ Resource Consultants Inc., which has operated a Superfund telephone hotline for the Environmental Protection Agency. The contractor answers questions from government agencies, industry, and the general public about arcane hazardous waste regulations. Hotline callers have rarely known that their inquiries were being answered by a private consultant instead of agency officials—a consultant that in many cases interpreted federal pollution laws on behalf of the Environmental Protection Agency. The General Accounting Office recently told the EPA that such functions, because of their interpretive nature, should be performed by government workers.

Underdone oversight. One of the most troublesome aspects of the Shadow Government is a lack of proper contractor oversight by federal agencies. In many instances, contracting budgets have grown faster than budgets for awarding and monitoring contracts. Agencies, such as the Energy Department, the EPA, NASA, and the Defense Department during the 1980s, saw tremendous increases in contractor work forces with little corresponding gain by agency units charged to watch over them.

The General Accounting Office and the agency's inspectors general have blasted the government for making poor, often illegal contracting awards and for ignoring conflict of interest questions. Inadequate oversight has led to dozens of cases in which agencies overpaid contracts, often by millions of dollars, and awarded unjustified contracts that violated federal law. Fraud, waste, and abuse by contractors is not uncommon in such an environment, since agencies simply lack the resources to catch or crack down on their errant contractors. It was in this environment, for instance, that NASA in the late 1980s discovered that some of its subcontractors had been fabricating test results for critical bolts used for the space shuttles.[14]

A clear case of insufficient oversight involves the Hubble Telescope that NASA launched into space in 1990. Not until this eye on the universe was in orbit did scientists discover a contractor's imperfectly made mirror had rendered the telescope seriously myopic. Indeed, a panel of former government scientists and outside experts who reviewed the manufacture of the telescope's mirrors concluded that the space agency had been overwhelmed by the task, and that NASA's oversight had been hampered by budget constraints and personnel ceilings.[15]

Federal brain drain. More than a decade of government contracting out some of its most important functions has eroded the considerable technical expertise once present in the federal agencies. Senior civil servants, already discouraged by salaries uncompetitive with the private sector, have left their agencies as the choicest work assignments have been handed over to contractors. A vicious cycle often results, as agencies losing their capability to perform technical tasks or to monitor

and evaluate the contractors on whose work they rely, end up
contracting out even more federal tasks.

One union, the National Federation of Federal Employees,
has complained that EPA's Office of Toxic Substances in the late
1980s had contracted out virtually every staff function in the
office. Only the director and a few other people remained. And
the Resolution Trust Corp. (RTC), in its rush to sell off nearly
$300 billion in real estate and other assets to pay off federal
costs in the bailout of the savings and loan industry, has created the largest private sector contracting bonanza ever seen in
the real estate management field. The RTC sought to avoid mistakes made by other government agencies by hiring several
dozen "contracting cops" to act as an early warning system for
federal law enforcement officials. The RTC's inspector general
office has hired some 150 auditors and investigators to help
guard against fraud. Nonetheless, several of the federal agency's private property management contractors already have
been involved in questionable and illegal practices.

Reliance on contractors for critical government tasks not only
raises questions of interest conflicts and accountability, but also
makes it increasingly difficult for federal agencies to maintain
independence from the private companies they employ. Agencies most dependent on federal contractors often have found
themselves captives to the consultants. The Energy Department, for instance, continued awarding bonuses to contractors
even though their workers had been involved in the toxic contamination of weapons production facilities. NASA gave Hubble contract managers high ratings for meeting only minimal
standards on performance—and may have paid the companies
that built the myopic telescope as much as $1 million in re-
wards for their cost-cutting efforts.[16]

Loss of Expertise in Government

During the 1980s, as technical talent left the government, agencies were suddenly without the expertise needed to evaluate
contractor work. Moreover, as many critical tasks were parceled out to contractors, technical staff remaining at the agencies became responsible for monitoring contracts. Many of the
government's engineers and scientists were suddenly watch-

ing others do their work. Many federal technical experts say they have little choice but to work for contractors themselves if they want to practice the occupations in which they were educated.

The combination of declining federal technical abilities and cozy, long-term, noncompetitive contracts also forces federal agencies into crippling dependencies on private companies. Agencies find themselves in situations where only one corporation can provide services required by the government. In such instances only that contractor, neither the agency nor other contractors, has the expertise and institutional memory to undertake the government's work. Not only are prices for such services typically exorbitant, but also should a sole-source contractor engage in fraudulent or abusive practices, an agency has considerable incentive to downplay any irregularities to ensure that the services continue uninterrupted.

In October 1989, for example, the Energy Department's procurement office sought a decision from Energy Undersecretary John C. Tuck on whether or not to approve a temporary contract with BDM for technical support to the department's Office of Defense Waste and Transportation Management. In a memo to Tuck, Procurement Director Berton J. Roth warned that continuing the BDM contract (funds for the contracted work had been used up ahead of schedule) would probably be seen by critics as an inappropriate extension of a sole-source contract. Roth also noted, though, that BDM's assistance was necessary to continue operating the defense waste office. He predicted that failure to approve the $3.6 million, six-month contract would have a "major impact" on the department.[17] Tuck, with little obvious choice, approved the contract extension the same day Roth's memo was written.

DEPARTMENTS' DETERIORATION

The Department of Energy (DOE)

As the Shadow Government expands, and limits on the number of civil servants persist, agency management suffers significantly. A case in point: The Department of Energy lost more than 4,000 employees during the 1980s as a consequence of Ronald Reagan's vow to dismantle the department. Today, with a staff of about 17,000, Energy manages a $17.7 billion budget, the majority of which is funneled to the department's more than 100,000 contractors. Three months after he was confirmed as secretary, James D. Watkins announced to Congress that the department he took over no longer had enough skilled employees capable of managing the government's contractor-run nuclear weapons program.[18]

Not only was this an extraordinary admission for any federal agency official, but it came at perhaps the most critical point in the Energy Department's history. Confidence in the department was at an all-time low after serious safety and environmental flaws were revealed at the government's nuclear weapons production plants. It will take some $200 billion and 30 years to clean up the radioactive and hazardous waste, and to provide safe working environments at the plants. And although it was DOE's inattention to contractors and operating details that led to many of the costly problems, contractors continue to perform most of the department's work. Contractors continue to operate Energy's weapons plants, contractors are handling much of the hazardous waste clean up, and contractors are carrying out many of the assessments that will determine what portions of antiquated weapons production facilities can be salvaged and be made safer.

How pervasive are private consultants in the federal government? At the Energy Department, at least, they are everywhere. "Virtually all DOE official documents embody the work product of contractors," concluded an investigation by the Senate Governmental Affairs Subcommittee on Federal Services, Post Office, and Civil Service.[19]

The Environmental Protection Agency (EPA)

Contractors dominate the Superfund program at the Environmental Protection Agency also. Managers at EPA have doled out between 80 and 90 percent of the cleanup program's funds to contractors, more than $8 billion since Superfund was created in 1981. For most of this period, as spending for contractors had escalated, the staff for EPA monitoring remained flat. Congress's Office of Technology Assessment reviewed the situation several years ago and its findings were devastating: "The EPA work force cannot effectively design, monitor, and evaluate contractor work, in large measure because it has too few technical workers with too little experience, and paid too little salaries."[20] What's more, OTA linked Superfund's poor record in cleaning up the nation's worst hazardous waste sites to EPA's "heavy dependence on contractors and limited technical ability to effectively control them."[21]

During the Bush administration, EPA under Administrator William K. Reilly has eliminated some consultants, brought their work back into the government, and added personnel to monitor contracting activities. Nonetheless, new environmental mandates, such as the Clean Air Act Amendments of 1991, a toughened air pollution law, are expected to increase the demand for consulting services as EPA races to meet a series of strict legislative deadlines for implementing the law.

The National Aeronautics and Space Administration (NASA)

The National Aeronautics and Space Administration (NASA) has struggled with similar problems. Though NASA's budget has increased by roughly 40 percent since the late 1980s, its personnel levels have risen by just 8 percent. Agency officials say that an equivalent increase in budget and personnel are not required, but a closer correlation is necessary. Demands on NASA continue to grow, yet its staffing has not kept up.

So again, the space agency turns to contractors. Though the number of NASA's contract engineers and scientists had remained roughly between 5,000 and 6,500 between 1972 and 1987, the agency's engineering contractors have more than doubled to 13,000 in the last three years.[22]

The pervasiveness of contractors and consultants in the everyday work of NASA is evident in the uneasiness many agency scientists and engineers express about the erosion of excellence in this once premier center of technical expertise. Though such feelings were known anecdotally for years, and have contributed to the departure of many talented engineers from the agency, a recent NASA study by the National Academy of Public Administration (NAPA) found the Shadow Government's debilitating presence in NASA facilities across the country. Some of NAPA's findings are:

- Two-thirds of NASA's senior scientists and engineers in the NAPA survey said the public interest would be best served if less technical work were contracted out to the private sector. More than 50 percent said that the future role of contractors should be more limited.[23]

- Only 22.5 percent thought that NASA's scientific and engineering capabilities are as strong now as in the past. By a ratio of 4:1, both NASA and its contractor managers believe that the agency's in-house technical capability has eroded over time.[24]

- More than 80 percent of NASA scientists and engineers surveyed said that the agency must do more to provide its technical personnel with opportunities to enhance their skills in order to effectively perform their work.[25]

Much of the work NASA does has grown not only in quantity but also in complexity. Expansion stems from the cargo-carrying capability of the space shuttle and an increase in defense and scientific payloads. However, the number of civil service scientists and engineers has declined at all but one of the agency's space centers engaged in NASA's traditional research, design, test, and evaluation tasks. As a result, NASA has been forced to shift much of its science and engineering staff into activities associated with launch operations, and away from core responsibilities at its development centers that once provided the space agency with its superb reputation.

THE FEDERAL RETAILERS

Contracting out, whether for services the government produces itself, or for goods and services that Washington cannot effectively produce on its on, represents a wholesale change in the philosophy of governing America. This penchant to purchase rather than to produce is just part of a growing change in what scholars call third-party government, or government by proxy. Both terms refer to a federal government grown dependent on local governments and on private and nonprofit organizations to provide Washington's services. The difference is that the services are directed at citizens, not federal agencies. The government has increasingly less contact with the citizenry as others implement the policies Washington formulates.

A Third-Party Government

The province of the proxies has grown ever larger as the government's role in society has continued to expand. In aid to the poor, the aged, and the sick, farmers and small businesses, and assistance to home buyers and the homeless, third parties support literally thousands of social programs.

Direct loans and guarantees, intergovernmental grants, tax expenditures, subsidies, and credits—all are offered to individuals by nonpublic and quasi-public entities on behalf of the federal government.

Most Americans have not caught on to this fundamental change in the nature of the government. Even fewer truly appreciate the magnitude of its growth in the past two decades, and the tax dollars such programs can consume to cover defaults when they fail. Indeed, only in the late 1980s did many Americans become familiar with what happens when a federally insured program fails: For years to come, taxpayers will be paying the multibillion-dollar costs of bailing out depositors of the nation's savings and loan banks.

One reason Americans generally are unaware of the extraordinary expansion of third-party government is because its costs are hidden deep inside the federal budget. Many of these indirectly funded programs, such as loans and insurance, are not listed as federal expenditures because they require no upfront money from the government. Such programs incur costs to the Treasury only when they fail.

By one estimate, Washington today spends only 15 percent of the budget on programs performed by its own civil servants,

including the military services.[26] Grants-in-aid to state and local governments, among the oldest of federal transfer programs, grew rapidly in the 1960s and 1970s. And while they
declined as part of the Reagan cutbacks in the 1980s, these
commitments still account for nearly 12 percent of all federal
spending.[27]

The Fast Expansion of Federal Loan and Credit Programs

Most astounding, however, has been the swiftness with which
federal loan and credit programs have expanded. The federal
government is the nation's largest supplier and guarantor of
credit. By 1990 the government was responsible for a whop-
ping $1.7 trillion in loans and credit, some 20 percent of the
U.S. total.[28] At the end of 1990, the face amount of federal and
federally assisted credit and insurance was $6.2 trillion, up 8
percent from 1989 and up 110 percent over 10 years.[29] The dollar value of federal credit and insurance grew 594 percent between 1970 and 1990, as deposit insurance increased 491
percent, loan guarantees advanced 404 percent, and loans from
government-sponsored enterprises soared an unprecedented
3,462 percent.[30]

Indeed, by 1990 the government had accumulated in loans
alone $210 billion in outstanding direct loans, $630 billion in
outstanding guarantees of private sector loans, and $855 billion
in outstanding loans or guarantees issued by government-
sponsored enterprises, those congressionally created private
businesses that make or repackage loans and sell them in specific markets with implicit federal backing.[31]

Growth in a Third-Party Government

The reasons for growth in third-party government are numerous and complex. Wariness of an overly powerful federal structure has encouraged politicians to limit Washington's reach;
yet that reach, even unfettered, can only extend so far and still
be successful during the kind of historic expansion in social
services this country has experienced in recent decades. Gov-

ernment truly would be enormous had it been forced to implement all the programs and policies possible in the modern welfare state by *itself*.

The shift to third-party government is also not without political motivations. It allows Congress and administrations the advantage of providing a variety of generous services to constituents without outwardly having to spend scarce federal dollars, without requiring tax increases, and—except for programs funded from tax expenditures—without raising the federal deficit. Such programs must seem almost free to politicians eager to dispense federal dollars. Such courses of action also are easy, since the government itself is basically free of a program's design, implementation, and outcome.

What the government is not free of, however, is accountability. Regardless of whether a public or private sector organization dispenses the government's largesse, Washington is still held responsible for the results. A loss of taxpayer funds resulting from waste, fraud, and abuse is just that—regardless of whose hand actually does the feeding.

The Government's Vulnerability to Private Companies

But in the programs administered by third parties, as with consultants and contractors, Washington has become vulnerable to unscrupulous private concerns cognizant that a beleaguered and short-staffed civil service is paying their activities scant attention. The Department of Education, for example, in recent years has lost billions resulting from student loan defaults. Guaranteed loans to students grew dramatically in number during the 1980s, and with that came an even higher increase in defaults. The federal government was left to make good with the guaranty agencies. Default payments rose to $2.48 billion in fiscal 1990 from just $144 million in fiscal 1980, a 1,600 percent increase.[32]

The story of the nation's S&Ls, of course, is a devastating example of programs gone awry. Since deregulation in the early 1980s, savings and loans have squandered billions of dollars in risky deals, knowing that depositors' funds were federally insured. Unfortunately, the incidence of fraud was rising at virtually the same time Reagan-era budget and personnel cuts at the federal banking agencies prevented the regulators from investigating abuses and stemming losses that ultimately caused the government to seize more than one-third of the country's thrift institutions.

The Department of Housing and Urban Development (HUD) may prove to be the classic example of the Shadow Government and the distribution of trillions of dollars in federal insurance and credit. HUD's losses are not so monumental as those so far exposed in the S&L scandal, but the debacle has as much to do with the decline of a cabinet department as it does with outright fraud and abuse.

Although HUD management has clearly learned some lessons from its scandal and has moved to eliminate some of the biggest abuses of the system, the underlying issue, inadequate staff to manage growing responsibilities, remains. And as long as this gap exists, so too does the opportunity for fraud to be repeated. Without attention to management and monitoring, HUD can be had—as can the entire government.

Chapter Seven

Aiding America

J ust west of Albany, New York, on a stretch of state highway near rural Amsterdam, a bridge collapsed over the Schoharie Creek in the spring of 1987, killing 10 people as cars and trucks plunged into the icy water.

CITIES' PUBLIC WORKS CRUMBLING

Certainly not all of America's bridges will collapse like the Schoharie span, but some will—unless the nation, especially the federal government, reverses its decades-long decline in spending for the nation's stock of highways and bridges, subways, waste systems, and other public works. It is not only just the bridges that need fixing, but the streets and highways, water systems, and transit lines as well. For example, New York City's streets and highways are crumbling and congested, its aging water lines are corroding and bursting, subway tunnels are caving in, and its sewer and water treatment facilities in many instances are now literally overflowing.

Cities all over America share New York's problems, though not always in size and scope. Philadelphia also has become poor physically. Parts of its drinking water and wastewater treatment plants are more than 100 years old and need extensive restorations. The transportation system, both the city's mass transit and its highways, are sorely underfunded. A 1985 study of Philadelphia's infrastructure concluded that the city was investing only 35 percent of the funds needed to maintain its streets and highways and 65 percent of the money required to run and repair the subway system. Overall, Philadelphia now has a 40 percent investment shortfall between the city's needs and expenditures.[1]

And it is not just the cities. As the nation has continued its migration to urban areas, rural regions have lost much of the tax base necessary to pay for repairs and renovations. Investment in rural highways and roads has not kept pace.

Across the nation, airports have been deluged by demand, and wastewater treatment facilities frequently do not comply with federal water pollution laws. Mass transit often is unreliable or, worse, unavailable.

AMERICA'S STORE OF PUBLIC WORKS

America owns and uses an extraordinary store of public works. There are nearly 4 million miles of highway carrying 175 million cars and trucks each year; mass transit conveys about 9 billion passengers annually; even railroads, that endangered species of transportation, today haul an ever-increasing load of passengers as its popularity rises among commuters and travelers frustrated with other means of transport in the crowded Northeast corridor.

Yet much of this infrastructure is at least 20 years old, and a troubling amount is considerably older—in some cases a century old. In urban areas especially, the bridges, highways, sewer plants, and subway tunnels on which the nation daily relies were built to accommodate the growing immigrant cities of our grandfathers. Around the turn of the century the nation's infrastructure grew enormously: In the 35 years before World War I, the number of waterworks grew from 1,800 to 10,000; sewer miles increased from 6,000 to 30,000; and mass transit miles jumped from 5,000 to 35,000.[2]

But the Great Age of Public Works is over. In short, America's public works and infrastructure—the highways, subways, airports, docks, inland waterways, bridges, and water treatment plants that stimulate commerce and encourage economic efficiency—are not being adequately maintained and are falling apart. What's worse, the $1 trillion needed to upgrade the country's infrastructure is unlikely to be found in the strapped public budgets of federal, state, and local governments.

Thus, just 200 years after a central government supplanted a loosely tied confederation of states—in part to overcome the terrible shape of colonial transportation—the United States has come full circle. Much of this nation's transportation system is again in terrible shape. Economists suggest that its deterioration seriously hinders the nation's productivity and economic development at a time when, competitively, the country can least afford it.

Decline of U.S. Public Works

The story of investment in our public works is a story of decline. Over the last 25 years, public works spending has declined relative to total government spending, the level of private investment, and the nation's total annual production of goods and services. A report on the state of the nation's infrastructure in 1988 concluded, "These trends suggest an inevitable imbalance between demand and supply that will eventually lower the level and quality of services being provided."[3]

Today the nation spends as a percentage of gross national product one-half of what was spent for nonmilitary public investment in the 1970s, and just one-quarter of what was spent in the 1950s and 1960s.[4] Indeed, economists increasingly blame neglected infrastructure for the nation's declining industrial competitiveness. By one estimate, the annual growth of productivity in the United States during the past 20 years was a lackluster 0.6 percent, compared to 1.8 percent in England, 2.3 percent in France, 2.4 percent in West Germany, and 3 percent in Japan.[5]

Indeed, the noted economist David Aschauer calculates that nearly 60 percent of the nation's slumping productivity can be attributed to "neglect of our core infrastructure."[6]

GOVERNMENT'S ROLE

An increasingly Hollow Government, possessing a shrinking pool of domestic discretionary funds and a growing budget deficit, has led to hollow public works. And today, the bill is coming due. To repair or replace an estimated 240,000 bridges will cost more than $50 billion. Just repairing and renovating the nation's highways could exceed $40 billion annually (calculated in 1982 dollars) until after the year 2000.[7] By one estimate, $118 billion annually will be required over 20 years to modernize the nation's public works system.[8]

Infrastructure Decreases; Social Programs Increase

Government, unfortunately, does not appear up to the challenge. Total real public works spending has increased in absolute terms, but has declined as a spending priority of federal, state, and local governments. Government spending on public works represented 19 percent of their budgets in 1950, but by 1985 had declined to 6.8 percent.[9] At the federal level, infrastructure spending declined in the 1970s as social programs grew, and shrunk still further in the 1980s to make room for interest payments and the defense buildup. Federal outlays for physical resources, one of the government's broad spending categories that include transportation, natural resources, and community development, have shrunk from 11 percent of the budget in 1980 to 7 percent in 1990. Recent reports suggest that it will fall further still to 4 percent by 1995.[10] Moreover, that portion of the federal budget attributable to investment in physical capital of all kinds has declined as a percentage of GNP from 4.4 percent in 1960 to 2.2 percent in 1992.[11]

Driven by the cuts in federal spending and an increasing absence of leadership and management by Washington, states with pressing needs to improve or build public works have taken on the task themselves. Many of them, however, have been unable to make up the gap left by declining federal aid, especially in light of state and local budget shortfalls; the problem has been compounded in older cities by an eroding economic base and in newer cities by an inability to keep up with the growing demand for public works services.

Overall the federal government's share of spending on infrastructure has declined from 5.5 percent of federal outlays in 1965 to 2.5 percent of outlays in 1990. And when federal funds for highways and airports are excluded, investment in infrastructure has fallen even further. Indeed, the neglect is worst in funding for mass transit, railroads, water treatment, and hazardous waste treatment facilities.

SURFACE TRANSIT

When it comes to transportation, the federal government has long favored the highway. The Interstate Highway System, begun by President Eisenhower in 1956, is 43,000 miles long and cost about $300 billion to create, 90 percent of which was paid for by Washington. Today the system is nearly complete and construction funds are being de-emphasized as repairs and renovations of the existing—and, after 35 years, deteriorating—system take a greater percentage of funds.

Lost Time—Highway Congestion, Gasoline Consumption

Yet just as this massive public works project winds down, engineers and traffic experts are worrying about the system's future. They expect the nation to add as much traffic to its highways in the next 30 years as it did in the past 32 years.[12] Americans idle away nearly 2 billion hours a year in urban traffic congestion; this lost time is expected to double by 2005. Likewise, 2 billion gallons of gasoline are consumed as traffic stalls, at a cost to the economy of close to $30 billion annually. Road congestion could triple in 15 years if trends remain unchanged, even if highway capacity is increased by 20 percent.[13]

Although the federal government spends more on highways than on any other mode of transportation, even here it has begun to back off its funding commitment. To its credit, Washington will spend more than $150 billion by 1996 on the nation's highways, up more than 40 percent from the last time Congress authorized highway programs. The bad news for communities in need of better roads is that the White House plans to cut the federal share of most projects, shifting more of the burden to states and to local governments—most of

which, as a result of the 1990–92 recession's depressed receipts, are struggling with their worst budget deficits in a decade. Washington plans to shed its share of the highway
investment burden from about 83 percent under existing rules
to nearly 72 percent in the future.

State and local government officials are concerned that they
will be unable to raise their share of highway funds, especially
since a majority of them have already raised gasoline taxes, the
main local revenue for highways. Neither is this revenue ave-
nue any longer wide open for Washington, which has tripled
the federal gas tax in less than 10 years.

Highways versus Mass Transit

What the government has spent on highways, however, it has
ignored on mass transit. Between 1981 and 1991, the federal
government cut mass transit funds by one-half. Indeed, a relatively small, but to local governments still welcome, increase
that is part of the new legislation is the first rise in transit funds
since the Carter administration. Even so, the mass transit budget is likely to remain virtually unchanged for five years. The
result is that some of the nation's nearly bankrupt systems
could end up in considerably worse shape.

What's more, the White House, in its belt-tightening efforts,
also wants to cut off federal operating funds for mass transit
systems, providing aid just for capital outlays. Cities such as
Philadelphia, New York, Detroit, and San Francisco could
wind up cutting operating hours, reducing trains, and eliminating station stops.

As part of its attempt to cut back on mass transit, the administration has also suggested funding the federal share entirely
through the highway trust fund and weaning the Urban Mass
Transportation Administration from general revenues. Such a
move would make it easier to keep under budget ceilings, but
local governments are concerned that mass transit's reliance on
just the trust fund would further impoverish subway systems.
Removing mass transit from general revenues would also eliminate an important source of funding that, because of budget
politics, would be nearly impossible to get back. In the mean-

time, states would encounter significant difficulties making up the loss of funds, especially if depressed business conditions in the near future persist or recur.

AIR TRAFFIC TROUBLES

The nation's airports are not in much better shape than the highways or mass transit systems. Congress has been stingy in spending the airport and airway trust fund, a dedicated source of revenue, similar to the highway trust fund, derived by taxing airline passenger tickets. With a rapid growth in the number of planes and passengers, and a virtual 15-year moratorium on new airport construction, congestion and capacity problems have significantly slowed air traffic service in many cities. Almost everyone who flies has stories to tell about excessive traffic jams; even the secretary of transportation has sat in runway traffic jams. In the first five months of 1990, for instance, air traffic delays in metropolitan New York rose by nearly 50 percent.[14]

Increasing Cost of Delays

According to recent estimates, delays cost scheduled air carriers almost $2 billion in extra operating expenses and passengers $3 billion in lost time each year.[15] Twenty-five percent of the problem comes from too much traffic for airports and not enough air traffic controllers to handle the work.[16] Indeed, if no capacity improvements are made, estimates are that by 1997, 17 of the nation's busiest airports could end up as congested as Chicago's O'Hare airport is today. With 100,000 hours of delay annually, O'Hare holds the country's record for air traffic congestion.[17]

Building more runways and airports, which would provide the greatest increase in capacity to the air traffic system, requires considerable new capital investments. The problem was partially fixed in 1990 when, as part of the Federal Aviation Administration's reauthorization, Congress agreed to let airports charge higher airline passenger fees, a potentially enormous source of revenue for financing expansions and modernizations.

Just the same, only a handful of the nation's most congested airports have such projects under way; most local communities have been unwilling to put up with increased noise and air pollution, and land-use changes that such expansions need. Furthermore, airport operators across the country have suggested that they will need to spend more than $50 billion by 1995 to keep up with the demand.[18] The new fees will provide just a fraction of this amount; the remaining money will come from the airlines, airport concessionaires, and other tenants.

Reduced Spending on Public Works

Not only has the federal government reduced its spending on the nation's deteriorating public works, but by diverting trust funds established to support infrastructure construction and maintenance, it also has broken a promise. Special trust funds paid for by taxes on gasoline and airplane tickets were created by Congress in the early 1970s to pay for infrastructure improvements. The gasoline tax has been used to fund highway repairs and renovations, and a share of passengers' airline ticket costs have flowed into the Airport and Airways Trust Fund to offset the costs of maintaining airports. As the federal deficit began to increase, however, Congress took to holding back portions of these dedicated taxes in order to cover the government's growing red ink.

The Airport and Airways Trust Fund

The Airport and Airways Trust Fund in fiscal 1991, for instance, took in nearly $1 billion more than it spent. The fund had a balance of $15.3 billion that Congress could have spent in 1991, and in recent years has been growing by about $1 billion annually.[19] Likewise, the Highway Trust Fund in fiscal 1991 brought $18.3 billion into the Treasury, but only spent $15.6 billion. The Highway Trust Fund balance is $21.2 billion and has grown by nearly $2 billion annually in recent years.[20] Indeed, for all of its trust funds in fiscal 1991, the government took in

$571.3 billion but spent just $453.1 billion on those designated programs—improving its cash flow by $118.2 billion.[21]

In 1990, the legislature stipulated that one-half of a new gasoline tax increase won't even go to the Highway Trust Fund at all. The inability of Congress to control spending and tackle the deficit has not only weakened domestic agencies, but also has weakened—at times literally—the physical fabric of the country.

ENVIRONMENTAL INVESTMENT

Finally, the government has in recent years neglected the vast investment necessary to build and maintain the nation's environmental public works, the wastewater treatment plants, drinking water plants, and solid waste facilities on which cities and towns rely. State and local governments, consequently, have been forced to pick up ever bigger portions of the bill.

Local Governments to Bear Burden of Improvements

At the same time that Washington has shirked much of its funding responsibilities, however, Congress has not been shy in imposing costs on others, mainly the local governments. New regulations designed to protect drinking water and enforce pollution laws are expected to cost billions of dollars at the local community level. There is little dispute that most of the federal government's environmental mandates will provide benefits in the long term, but its increasing inclination to make local communities bear the burden for improvements is part of an overall trend by which Washington, in recent years, has handed off its responsibilities without the commensurate resources to achieve the results.

Environmental regulations are costly. Public water systems alone will be forced to spend $553 billion by the year 2000 to comply with regulations mandated by the 1986 amendments to the Safe Drinking Water Act. Federal, state, and local governments in 1987 spent $40 billion for environmental protection, but simply to maintain the 1987 standards will cost $56 billion in the year 2000. The amount climbs to $61 billion if costs for new environmental regulations are figured in.[22]

The burden of these rising costs will fall predominantly on local governments, which are expected to pick up 87 percent of the public bill for sewers, drinking water, and waste management in 2000, up from 82 percent in 1987. Meanwhile, the state's share will remain steady at about 5 percent and the federal government's environmental public works spending will fall from 13 percent to 8 percent as Washington phases out wastewater treatment facility grants.[23]

Larger communities will have little trouble tapping into the bond market to raise their share of the estimated $19 billion in new capital that local governments will have to raise annually by the year 2000 to pay for environmental projects. Smaller communities with limited resources and less access to capital markets, along with older cities already struggling under significant debt burdens, could have trouble keeping up.

Consider some of the major environmental costs communities must shoulder in the coming years:

- More than $84 billion in capital investment will be needed to bring municipal wastewater treatment facilities into compliance with the Clean Water Act.[24] Local communities need to construct and renovate sewer systems to comply with laws regulating damaging runoff problems. Regulations on toxic waste, sludge disposal, and wetlands protection are likely to impose additional costs as well.

  Federal grants have played an important role in developing wastewater treatment plants, but as with so many other things, in recent years Washington has backed off its commitment. Federal construction grants in the early 1980s averaged $4 billion annually and supplied about one-half of all investment in wastewater facilities. Beginning in 1989, however, construction grants were replaced by Washington with grants to capitalize state revolving funds. The new grants expire in 1994, presumably along with the federal government's responsibility for the country's wastewater treatment facilities. The grants-turned-revolving funds will still leave many states considerably short in meeting local investment needs: Even if states are able to leverage their capitalization grants, at least 20 of them face combined financing needs of nearly $57 billion.[25]

- Compliance with safe drinking water regulations will require states to absorb an estimated 50 percent increase in annual outlays for water supplies.[26] The majority of costs will be imposed through efforts to meet the Environmental Protection Agency's regulations on surface water filtration, controlling contaminants, and keeping distribution systems maintained. Of particular concern are smaller communities, where more than one-half the expected capital investments must be made. Small drinking water systems, lacking the funds available to the big cities, often end up with the highest number of federal drinking water environmental violations.

- The cost of solid waste collection, construction, and operation of landfills and incinerators is expected to rise about 60 percent, from approximately $6 billion in 1987 to $9.6 billion in 2000. Existing landfills are reaching capacity at the same time that federal regulations have grown stricter and increased the costs for local governments both to operate old ones and open new ones, especially as the EPA completes rules for gas pollutants and incinerator ash.

AIDING CITIES

Public works are not the only part of the nation's infrastructure that the federal government has neglected. Washington backed away from new Great Society-type programs beginning in the mid-1970s, and this was followed by the conservative Republican politics of the 1980s. The result: A hollow federal government has precipitated a nation of hollow state and local governments.

As the 1980s turned into the 1990s, governments at all levels in America were cutting services to cope with budget deficits even though demands for services continued to rise. States haven't the resources or powers of the central government. Except for Vermont, states cannot legally run deficits to wait out recessions that rob them of revenues. Thus, most states have no choice but to raise taxes to offset budget shortfalls, an action that often is a death knell for elected local politicians who are held closely accountable for the communities' living conditions.

States' Crises in Public Services

In reducing resources to states and local governments during a period of considerable growth, Washington clearly has contributed to the crisis in public services that many communities are now experiencing. For almost two decades, rising fiscal needs at the local level had been eased by federal funds. Great Society programs, General Revenue Sharing, hundreds of grants and other forms of federal aid helped cities struggle against the persistent growth in urban poverty, inadequate housing and homelessness, crime, drugs, high school dropouts, and illegal immigrants—the ever rising tide of the cities' troubles.

Decrease in Federal Assistance

But is was not to last. The highpoint of federal assistance to the states was 1978, after which citizens through their local communities received a dwindling share of Washington's largesse. By that point, writes Robert Reischauer, former director of the Congressional Budget Office, Great Society programs had fully run their course, finally done in by both their successes and excesses.[27] And while Jimmy Carter sought an alternative urban policy, he never quite found one; instead, the void was filled by Ronald Reagan's New Federalism, which all but turned the Great Society on its head.

Reagan's idea of intergovernmental relations was to return to the states responsibilities that over several decades had accrued to Washington. The states readily agreed, sensing in the proposition a chance to control at the local level greater resources, to dole out, and to get the credit for more federal benefits distributed to their communities.

Reagan failed to mention, however, that in turning back the responsibilities to the states, local governments would in many instances not be getting the federal funds necessary to efficiently and equitably run the programs. In effect, Washington was simply shedding the problems, thus removing the weight from its own overburdened budget.

The results largely were disastrous—a calculated federal disinvestment clearly evident in the numbers:

- Between 1978 and 1988, federal grants-in-aid as a percentage of total state-local outlays declined from 26.5 percent to an estimated 17.1 percent; as a percent of federal outlays, they shrunk from 17 percent to roughly 10.4 percent; and as a percentage of the gross national product, federal grants-in-aid declined from 3.6 percent to an estimated 2.3 percent. Meanwhile, the number of federal grant programs was cut from 492 to about 435.[28]
- A decade ago, cities counted on the federal government to provide about 18 percent of their budgets, but by 1990 Washington was contributing only 6 percent of the funds in 50 urban areas. One result is that cities, which raised about 65 percent of their own funds at the beginning of the Reagan administration, now must come up with about 75 percent of their budget.[29]
- In 1978, intergovernmental transfers from the federal government made up some 9 percent of local government revenues, but by 1987 it was just 4.2 percent.[30]

At the same time, several major programs providing funds for local communities were cut in the increasingly harsh budget battles that characterized Congress's Gramm-Rudman deficit reduction struggles. In 1986 General Revenue Sharing, a major source of unrestricted urban federal funding, was eliminated. In 1988 Congress scrapped another important tool for cities, the Urban Development Action Grant (UDAG) program. The funds saved from UDAG were funneled to the jobs-and contract-rich National Aeronautics and Space Administration.

Bush Administration Lacks Interest in Urban Areas

Meanwhile, the Bush administration has shown little interest in improving the lot of American urban areas. Outside of a few high-profile programs such as Head Start, a $2 billion effort to ensure that economically disadvantaged children improve learning skills, White House and congressional attention has been lacking. Washington's urban policies have been heavy on slogans such as "empowerment" but light on new funds.

For example, the only new housing initiative in a decade, the National Affordable Housing Act of 1990, seeks in part to "empower" public housing tenants by helping them own their dwellings. This is a questionable proposition in the minds of many housing experts to begin with; equally important, the act provided scant funds to replenish the nation's dwindling stock of affordable housing units at a time when the homeless population continues to rise and the majority of local housing authorities have waiting lists for units. Furthermore, funds for the act were taken largely from other HUD housing programs. In the end, little new money was made available for what the Bush administration considered one of its significant 1990 legislative achievements.

Nevertheless, even had the Bush administration shown more concern about the plight of the nation's cities, the 1990 Budget Enforcement Act would have constrained any substantive initiatives. And therein lies the most depressing news for cities. The budget caps that limit domestic discretionary spending during the next several years all but guarantee that Washington will not be coming to their aid. Unless the "firewalls" between budget accounts are breached, the 1990 budget agreement prevents Washington from aiding cities at the time they need it most. Only by cutting other domestic programs can Congress now assist the country's urban centers.

Government Hands Over Responsibilities to Local Governments

Furthermore, starting in 1992 the Bush administration wanted to hand over more responsibilities to state and local governments. In a tradition begun by Richard Nixon and subverted by Ronald Reagan, federalism attempts to return vital public services to those governments closest to the constituencies receiving them. Federalism has its advantages in theory—it cuts overhead, encourages innovation, and gives flexibility to local governments—but in practice it has fared poorly. Congress has never been a big fan of federalism. After all, under federalism the states, not federal legislators, get the credit for doling out federal revenue.

Some $15 billion in federally funded programs, including rural health, education, highways, law enforcement, and job training, would have been returned to the states in the latest federalism bid. Governors for the most part endorsed the plan, although some have been skeptical because of the Budget Enforcement Act's impact. New Jersey's Democratic Governor James J. Florio told a reporter from *The Washington Post*, "We're dealing with an artificial situation. . . . Do you want more discretion? Of course you do. But discretion to deal with less money? That's not doing us a favor."[31]

New Form of Federalism

Mayors generally have been less enamored with the newest version of federalism. Many have objected to proposals by the National Governors Association and other state-level organizations to fold the domestic programs into block grants, because under those circumstances there is no guarantee that the bulk of federal funds would end up in urban areas where the needs are greatest.

Congress rejected the most recent attempts to unload programs onto the states, but what's particularly worrisome about such attempts by Washington to pass the buck is that nearly four-fifths of the programs selected by the Bush administration serve the poor. They include $3 billion for low-income housing, roughly the same for social services, and nearly $5 billion for administering programs such as Medicaid and welfare. The not insignificant risk inherent in such programs is that governors could divert funds to concerns and programs favored by those constituencies better heeled than the poor. Funds once spent on social services for the needy could quickly be redirected to, say, solid waste disposal or other services of more benefit to a more powerful and voting middle-class community.

Future Support by the Government

In the meantime, Congress and the White House have continued the dubious tradition of handing off new responsibilities to the states without commensurate increases in funding to pay for them.

State governments once hailed as "laboratories" for innovation have become less eager to carry on that distinction as federal revenues have dwindled—and unfunded mandates from Washington haven't. Indeed, in the last few years a raft of federal regulations and orders have required states to take on new responsibilities in everything from Medicaid to air quality standards enforcement, often without the flexibility or cash to administer the programs.

THE MEDICAID BURDEN

These days, the mandate with the steepest price tag is Medicaid, a joint federal-state program that provides health services to the poor. Since 1987 Congress has required states to give Medicaid coverage to more pregnant women, infants, and young children, as well as to some elderly Medicare beneficiaries with low incomes. Then in 1988 Congress expanded coverage to families leaving welfare for jobs. New coverage for the poor and elderly was added in 1990 and 1991.

States are struggling under the Medicaid burden. The National Governors Association reports that Medicaid spending in 1980 accounted for 9 percent of state budgets, yet had risen to 14 percent by 1990. Estimates are that states will spend about $66 billion to fulfill the ever-expanding Medicaid mandates in 1995, more than double the $31.4 billion they spent in fiscal 1990.[32]

By the end of the 1980s, federal grant reductions, combined with the growing mandates, had begun to squeeze the budgets of the local communities. However, the problem was made worse by the recession that dried up tax revenues. The American economy slid to a stop by mid-1990, declining after seven years of growth, the longest peacetime expansion in U.S. history.

Impact of Recession on Budget Deficits

The recession has had a profound impact on tax receipts for state and local government. As the economy began to slow down in 1989, cities and states throughout the country started experiencing budget shortfalls; the projected revenue to fund services didn't materialize. Within months, many states were announcing budget deficits—the result of lower revenues, increasing service demands, and stiffer mandates. Minnesota is a good example: Though revenues were falling and the budget was expected to increase just 1 percent, its costs for Medicaid were climbing by 25 percent.

Thirty states were forced to raise taxes in 1989, many doing so for the first time since the end of the 1982 recession. Most states have no choice in the matter, for every state but Vermont is governed by laws prohibiting public sector budget deficits. Even after raising taxes, however, states quickly saw that the tax hikes were insufficient to maintain services and prevent deficits.

More than one-half of the cities and states in America were spending more than they took in. By 1991 one out of every four city governments was facing a budget gap of more than 5 percent. Among cities in the 100,000 to 300,000 population range, revenues declined an average 4.2 percent. Overall city per capita expenditures grew by 5.5 percent in 1991, while revenues were expected to grow just 2.2 percent.[33] The results of this fiscal crisis have made headlines. In 1991 California was facing more than $14 billion in shortfalls; New York state had $6 billion in red ink; and New York City, some 15 years after its brush with bankruptcy, was $3.5 billion short.

Cities and States Hard Hit

States also have been hit hard. The 1991 state budgets, adjusted for inflation, grew on average an estimated 1 percent, the slowest growth since the end of the 1982 recession. And with the recession in full swing, spending for welfare and for unemployment compensation swiftly rose. All told, states were faced with more than $44 billion in red ink. As a result, states have been enacting current services budgets that provide for few, if any, new initiatives, have continued to enact steep spending cuts, and have cut their own bureaucracies by some 50,000 workers. Connecticut and Maine were forced to shut down the government altogether until legislators could agree on enough spending cuts and tax hikes to pass their budgets. In 1991, still rising budget demands dwarfed the more than $8 billion that 29 states had cut out of their enacted budgets and the $10.3 billion in taxes raised by 26 states.

Big Tax Hikes

Not surprisingly, the combination of big tax hikes and sizable cuts in services is politically risky for any elected official, but mayors and governors are especially vulnerable because of the greater impact local services, as opposed to federal programs, have on communities. Thus, many officials are particularly angry at Washington not only for paying little attention to their plight, but for pre-empting their ability to raise taxes. The federal government not only has taken away its support of the cities, but has increasingly crippled their abilities to support themselves.

Rather than enact property tax increases, a measure sure to precipitate middle-class hostility, local governments have typically sought to raise taxes on gasoline, cigarettes, and alcohol. But in the past few years, Uncle Sam beat them to it as part of Washington's desperate grab for deficit-paring revenues wherever they could. State sales taxes are rising, and states without income taxes are in some instances changing their minds—to the reluctant acquiescence of citizens. And more than a few states are seeing the beginnings of citizen tax revolts similar to those guided 15 years ago by California's Howard Jarvis. Thus, the latitude for continued tax increases is not great.

And so a decade of neglect, the 1980s, has come face to face with a decade of needs, the 1990s: Despite deficits, demands keep rising; not surprisingly, the result is Hollow Government. State and local politicians, instead of providing constituents new services for which they were elected, are instead presiding over the dismantling of a nearly 30-year legacy committing public expenditures to America's cities. Instead of doing more for the growing numbers of the poor, the immigrants, the homeless, the uneducated, and the elderly, cities and states are curtailing existing services and deciding not to provide many new ones. In 1991, 11 state governors proposed or implemented layoffs and 7 states either proposed or implemented furloughs; meanwhile, 24 reduced their budgets, 22 implemented hiring freezes, and 19 froze travel for state officials.[34]

State and Local Governments Staggering

The scope, severity, and suddenness of America's Hollow Governments has left state and local governments staggering. Consider some examples:

- In June of 1991, the city of Bridgeport, Connecticut, filed for bankruptcy, becoming the nation's first large urban center to take such drastic action. The ongoing recession, a virtual disappearance of the region's manufacturing tax base, and a steady decline in federal and state aid had drastically reduced the city's revenues at a time when unemployment, violent crime, and the infant mortality rate were straining Bridgeport's services. Though a federal court judge later blocked the city's bid for bankruptcy, the dramatic move highlighted the severe plight in which the old, industrial center found itself.

  Indeed, by the time Republican Mayor Mary C. Maron announced the decision to declare bankruptcy, Bridgeport already had curtailed many local public services in a desperate attempt to cut spending. The city eliminated such normal expectations of city dwellers as street cleaning, snow removal, and recreation; it also closed libraries and parks—all to no avail.

- City construction and repairs have been frozen. Sacramento, California, cannot afford to open its new main library, and Salt Lake City, Utah, is not able to build a fire station for a growing neighborhood. Honolulu, Hawaii, is slashing road repairs, and New York City is deferring maintenance on bridges and tunnels, many of which already are on the brink of being unsafe.

- Services for the poor have been cut. Higher food prices and rising needs resulting from the recession have forced local governments to stop providing food to thousands of undernourished children. In Maryland, for instance, 15 percent of the people receiving food benefits in 1991 were cut from the nutrition program because federal funding has not kept pace with food prices or demands. In many cases, new applications aren't even being taken. In Minnesota, legislators cut several health and mental health programs for children, while Georgia has frozen the number of caseworkers assigned to child abuse, even though the reported number of cases more than doubled in that state during the 1980s.

- In 1990 California eliminated nearly $300 million in cost-of-living adjustments for welfare recipients, the aged, and the disabled, and reduced funds to counties by $708 million, which forced the closure of, among other things, several mental health facilities. As the economy weakened further, so did the state's budget. California in 1991 suffered a deficit nearly four times larger than it did in 1990, forcing the state to consider serious service cuts, as expenditures have continued to outstrip revenues.

  Indeed, what the state's Republican Governor Pete Wilson calls the "structural deficit" has been growing for several years. Since 1985, for instance, expenditures for prisons have risen nearly 200 percent, medical insurance by 120 percent, welfare has grown 115 percent, and public school funding has increased 70 percent. General tax revenues at the same time have risen 60 percent in an attempt to pay for the out-of-control budget, but it clearly hasn't been enough.[35]

Barring a quick economic turnaround or extensive tax increases that would in themselves harm prospects for growth, the near-term future of cities is not a healthy one. Cuts in state and local budgets, unfortunately, may well continue for several years if the recession and extraordinary demand for services persist. However, the new initiatives necessary to solve the communities' growing problems with drugs, crime, homelessness, and education will find little funding from city councils and state legislatures. Needless to say, little additional assistance will be forthcoming from Washington, as the federal government continues to fight its own deficit reduction battle.

Chapter Eight
Inside Agencies

T ap the federal government almost anywhere, and the ring is hollow. Ineffective management and rapid turnover among political appointees stall and cripple programs, leading to poor morale and high turnover in the civil service. Program budget and personnel cuts, contracting out, low pay, and better career opportunities have discouraged the best and brightest, leaving fewer, less experienced agency employees to handle a growing number of complex responsibilities.

This chapter examines the impact of Hollow Government on four specific agencies—the Department of Housing and Urban Development (HUD); the Internal Revenue Service (IRS); the Consumer Product Safety Commission (CPSC); and the National Park Service (NPS)—and how, ultimately, the government has failed the people.

DEPARTMENT OF HOUSING AND URBAN DEVELOPMENT (HUD)

Crowds quieted when gavels banged down on committee room tables in the United States Senate and the House of Representatives in May of 1989. The Congress, belatedly, was beginning to investigate how a cabinet department had lost billions of dollars to waste, fraud, and abuse over the previous decade.

The HUD Scandal

The investigation of a scandal at the Department of Housing and Urban Development promised to be high political drama. It became news not only because of the allegations of wrongdoing against a member of the president's cabinet, and not only because Washington was abuzz with the apparent influence peddling by powerful Republicans, but because Congress had been warned of these misdeeds years previously, and had done nothing.

Much of the fraud and abuse perpetrated by politically connected Republicans and by little-watched private sector contractors probably would have happened regardless of the rundown condition in which HUD found itself by the end of the 1980s. Unfortunately, the subversion of housing programs for the benefit of developers, former department officials, and influential Republicans was made all the easier because of the Hollow Government.

By the time Ronald Reagan became president in 1981, a federal housing agency had existed for nearly 50 years, a legacy of the government's effort in the 1930s to repair the depression's economic destruction. Even through the Republican presidency of Richard Nixon, HUD had helped poor and lower-income Americans to obtain adequate housing and to improve urban living conditions.

HUD's mission originally was to provide "a decent home and a suitable environment for every American family."[1] Congress in 1968 quantified that goal, requiring HUD to provide 26 million units of housing within 12 years, including 6 million units for low- and moderate-income families.[2] HUD's efforts waxed and waned as Congress and various administrations refocused federal housing initiatives. The 1968 goal was never met, and ultimately abandoned. Nearly a quarter-century later, Congress appears to have little interest in setting housing policy by the numbers. Recent legislation has returned the department's focus to helping the poor find adequate housing.

HUD's budget and personnel cut. In the 1980s, however, even goals were largely absent at the housing agency. Simply put, the Reagan administration sacked HUD. Philosophically opposed to a federal role in the provision of affordable housing and bent on reducing the size of the government's bureaucracy, the Reagan administration sharply cut HUD's budget and personnel. Budget authority at HUD during the decade was cut by 80 percent and personnel was reduced by more than 20 percent.[3] HUD's budget authority was cut from an average of $27.5 billion a year in the period 1977 to 1981 to less than $9 billion a year between 1986 and 1989. At the same time, the department's staff was reduced from 15,697 in 1981 to 12,932 in 1989.[4]

The impact was devastating on the agency and on those Americans who counted on federal benefits and public housing for their basic needs. The number of households needing low-rent units has grown from 11.9 million in 1983 to a projected 14.3 million in 1993. Meanwhile, the number of low-rent housing units available has declined from 12.9 million in 1983 to an expected 10.6 million in 1993.[5]

Decline in budget authority. The decline in budget authority is partly explained by a shift from new construction to filling existing housing. Significantly, it also was a product of the Reagan administration's redefinition of what constituted a low-income family, a change that slowed the rate at which eligible families were added to the rolls each year. Their numbers shrank from 300,000 families per year in the late 1970s to approximately 100,000 per year a decade later.[6] As a result, the nation lost ground in housing during the 1980s, as rents increased and more tenants were forced to spend larger percentages of their income for shelter.

Cutting Staff

Reagan-era personnel cuts did much to destabilize HUD. And for a department responsible for about $296 billion in mortgage insurance, in hindsight it is not surprising that fraud, waste, and abuse flourished. Field offices were hit particularly hard, seriously reducing the department's ability to inspect or investigate projects supported by HUD or Federal Housing Administration (FHA) funds. As a result, there was no assurance that adequate services were being maintained or that subsidies for housing units were not being overpaid.

Mortgage approval delayed. Without an adequate field staff, HUD also was unable to evaluate the affordable housing market and the characteristics of people occupying public housing—thus further complicating the agency's efforts to formulate a public policy.

Procedural delays increased as staffing declined. During the mid-1980s, HUD mortgage approvals for many multifamily housing projects took up to two years, making them unattractive to investors and builders. What's more, lenders and builders frequently complained that HUD staffers could not interpret regulations because they had little experience with insurance and mortgage finance.

Loss of qualified career employees. HUD lost many of its most qualified career employees during the 1980s. As it became clear to the department's veterans that the Reagan administration would block and dismantle federal housing programs, veterans resigned to take higher paying private sector positions. Many had joined HUD during the department's formation in the mid-1960s out of an interest and commitment to affordable housing, but the cuts at HUD were the last straw to civil servants already disillusioned by stagnant federal salaries and the public's increasingly harsh attitude toward the bureaucracy. Field offices not only suffered from a shortage of staff to cover critical programs, but much of the work force they did have was inexperienced and inadequate to manage complex, fraud-ridden programs. Conditions had so deteriorated by 1985 that 22 percent of the staff at HUD field offices had been in their job for less than one year, and 25 percent of all supervisors in the appraisal and underwriting area had less than one year's experience.[7]

The coinsurance program. Staff reductions were further responsible for the fraud and abuse afflicting the multifamily coinsurance program, and which ultimately cost taxpayers more than $1 billion in federal losses. As part of the Reagan administration's privatization efforts, HUD in 1983 handed over to the private sector its coinsurance program. Privatized coinsurance financed multifamily housing for low- and moderate-income families, even though the government retained most of the program's risks. Indeed, from 1983 to 1986, the first three years of coinsurance's existence under private management, not a single HUD employee monitored the nearly $10 billion program.[8] Only after the president of the Mortgage Bankers Association of America complained to then-HUD Secretary Samuel Pierce Jr. of "unsound project underwriting and insufficient management oversight" of the coinsurance program did the department establish an oversight unit.[9] But Pierce created a token monitoring organization that even at the height of the scandal had less than a dozen people overseeing the entire coinsurance program.[10]

Robin HUD. HUD's lax scrutiny of its private escrow agents led to the now-fabled fraud of Marilyn L. Harrell, aka Robin HUD, who walked off with $6 million in federal funds. Ironically, HUD officials had adequate warning that its programs were at risk. The inspector general had issued reports pointing out management and oversight problems, and the department's regional administrators raised concerns in a 1986 report. The regional administrators concluded: "The quality of work performed by fee personnel as well as the quality of HUD's review of their work [have been] declining due to recent staff cuts which made acceptable levels of HUD involvement impossible. . . . When the quality goes down, the risk to the Department in terms of rate of default increases."[11]

Political Dumping Ground

At the same time the Reagan administration was cutting HUD's professional staff, the White House was compounding the damage by using the department as a personnel dump site. HUD, more than most other cabinet departments, was the repository for influential Republicans and campaign faithful who embraced the president's political conservatism. Few had management or housing experience.

High turnover in political ranks. HUD's programs also suffered more than those of other agencies because of extraordinarily high turnover in its political ranks. Ten people held the position of assistant secretary for housing/federal housing commissioner during the eight years of Ronald Reagan's presidency. But where political appointees stay in office two years or less, HUD Secretary Pierce, ironically, was the sole Reagan cabinet member to serve two full terms. Investigations into Pierce's involvement in HUD's scandals continue—and while no evidence has surfaced of personal gain from the department's housing project awards—at the least, the secretary was a disengaged manager who appears to have steered project funds toward influential Republicans and former top agency officials.

Dubois Gilliam, former HUD deputy assistant secretary for program policy development and evaluation, who was convicted during the scandal of conspiracy to defraud the government, told Congress: "I never should have been hired at HUD. . . . Samuel Pierce got loaded up on him a group of young Turks who were very political and on a must-hire list and we had no housing experience whatsoever."[12]

Political appointees rank third highest. During the 1980s, HUD had the third-highest percentage of political appointees in its career ranks of any cabinet department. When presidential appointments requiring Senate confirmation are added to political positions existing in the career ranks, an average of 30 percent of all HUD's top-management positions during the 1980s were awarded as patronage. Senior career management positions taken over by political appointees increased from 19.4 percent in 1979 to a high of 35 percent in 1984; the average was 24 percent at HUD for the decade as a whole. Similarly, political employees also infiltrated the ranks of career middle management at HUD, growing by roughly 50 percent between 1979 and 1988.[13]

The unprecedented increase of inexperienced political appointees contributed to the departure of experienced civil servants. It led to a decline in morale and skillful management at HUD, and was responsible for the ethical vacuum in which many project-funding decisions were made. Time after time, senior political appointees, including Deborah Gore Dean, Secretary Pierce's special assistant, appeared to make funding decisions which ran counter to the bureaucracy's professional advice, and which benefited influential Republicans and former HUD officials.

Financial Futility

Although overshadowed by political favoritism and inexperience compounded by staff shortages, many of HUD's problems can also be blamed on the perennial mismanagement of federal finances that seems endemic to government agencies.

Problems at HUD went largely unnoticed because adequate management controls simply did not exist. Relying in large part on antiquated paper files scattered throughout the country, HUD was unable to provide senior managers with timely, accurate information to help them track growing liabilities in its housing programs.

Political managers lax in duties. Making matters worse was the attitude of HUD's senior political managers who, when faced with reports of losses or abuses in the department's programs, tended to downplay their significance and rarely took actions to improve deteriorating situations. For example, HUD's administrators initially refused to report that the department's lax monitoring of coinsurance lenders violated its own regulations or that, as a result of improper controls, owners of Moderate Rehabilitation projects were being overpaid. HUD's inspector general Paul A. Adams (now retired) and his staff then tightened their audits of the department's activities, and reports took on a strident tone. In some cases, Adams could get HUD's management to admit to financial problems only after he had submitted written reports that essentially documented it for them.

Nonetheless, HUD's political managers were not the only people in Washington who ignored the warnings of the department's inspector general. Members of Congress and their staff paid Adams's reports little attention. Indeed, the chairmen of the very committees who seemed so indignant when hearings were finally convened, for several years had been receiving reports from the inspector general that warned them about the growing mismanagement in HUD's housing programs. But almost no one read them.

In a rare criticism of Congress's own performance, the Senate subcommittee investigating the HUD scandal suggested that the legislature's common neglect of executive branch management in favor of new programs with voter appeal contributed to the mess. Poorly crafted legislation and a propensity for Congress to frequently change HUD's focus made effective program management difficult—even if there had been competent, professional leadership.

INTERNAL REVENUE SERVICE (IRS)

Almost every year at budget time, Congress goes through a charade. As it struggles to find the funds necessary to bridge the budget deficit, the legislature decrees that the Internal Revenue Service (IRS) must collect more than it did the previous year.

Increasing Collections

The five-year budget agreement. As part of its 1990 five-year budget agreement, for instance, Congress ordered the IRS to come up with $9.4 billion more than the $5.5 trillion the agency was planning to collect by the end of fiscal 1995. In the meantime, the expected revenue was added to budget calculations, decreasing the deficit by $9.4 billion.

The trouble is, it is doubtful the U.S. Treasury will ever find the money. Past performance indicates that the IRS probably will be unable to collect the funds. The Congressional Budget Office (CBO) and independent tax experts say that the IRS cannot be counted on to squeeze any more money from delinquent taxpayers than the agency already gets.

Huge growth in budget and personnel. When it comes to Hollow Government, the IRS defies the standard model. Unlike most domestic agencies, the IRS in the 1980s experienced tremendous growth in budget and personnel, yet at the same time suffered a crippling decline in productivity. The result is:

less taxes collected and potentially higher deficits. The sorry state of affairs at the IRS can be summed up in a few statistics:

- A 42 percent increase in the agency's staff between 1981 and 1991, accompanied by a 48 percent real rise in the purchasing power of its budget, has not produced a commensurate increase in tax collections. The agency's budget increased from $2.5 billion in 1981 to $6.1 billion in 1991, while the number of employees rose from 84,700 to 120,000.[14] Nevertheless, revenues, adjusted for inflation, are up just 17 percent.
- Revenue collected per IRS employee, though rising nominally from $7.07 million to $9.75 million, between 1981 and 1991 actually declined in real terms.[15]
- Productivity at the tax collection agency declined by 17 percent in the past decade, while productivity in the nonfarm private sector grew by more than 12 percent.

The reasons for plummeting productivity include a growing work load, an increasingly complex business environment that leads to more complicated corporate tax cases, and the IRS's inability to invest for the long term. In the 1990s, for instance, IRS agents still labor on an antiquated computer system based on the technology of the 1950s.

Collections Backlog

One of the IRS's biggest problems is its inability to arrest an upward trend in uncollected taxes. In fact, IRS accounts receivable (i.e., taxes, penalties, and interest that have been assessed but not yet paid) rose to $66 billion in fiscal 1989, up from $26 billion in 1983.[16]

The IRS writeoffs. Unfortunately, billions owed the government by deadbeat citizens may never be collected. The General Accounting Office (GAO) reports that much of the current backlog of receivables, perhaps more than half, is probably lost forever. Some of the debt is not really owed, and is on the books because of IRS or taxpayer error. Another portion of the accounts receivable will never be collected because the delinquent taxpayers have gone bankrupt. Others have outrun the six-year statute of limitations. As a result, the IRS recently was forced to write off more than $20 billion in back taxes it had been trying to collect—more than twice the amount Congress is demanding the IRS add to its collections by 1995.

Equally troubling, the GAO reports, is that the inventory of accounts receivable increased by $13.6 billion (32 percent) between fiscal 1986 and 1989, and the number of delinquent accounts rose by 2.7 million in the same period. Moreover, the accounts receivable are getting older, which means they are increasingly harder to collect. In fiscal 1989, more than 55 percent of the accounts were more than one year old, compared to 46 percent of the inventory in fiscal 1986.

Tax debts uncollectible. While the agency's cumulative inventory of reported but uncollected tax debts grew to $66 billion in fiscal 1990, at least another $100 billion goes uncollected each year—nearly enough money to eliminate the federal deficit in three years. This $100 billion funding gap represents money that Americans simply don't report as earned income to the IRS. It is income earned in off-the-books transactions between vendors and purchasers in the underground economy. Many delinquents are small-time operators—sole proprietors, street vendors, and workers who depend on tips. And roughly 25 percent are corporations that mischaracterize their income or abuse deductions.

Tax gap cut slightly. The IRS computer matching program, which reviews taxpayer returns for consistency with corporate payroll, dividends, and other reports, has cut the tax gap somewhat among individual tax filers. But understandably it has not been able to tap into the underground economy. In fact, the IRS believes uncollected taxes will rise to $127 billion in 1992, an estimate that does not include income from such illegal activities as narcotics trafficking and illicit gambling.

It doesn't help that the agency's rate of auditing individual taxpayers has been steadily dropping for more than a decade and is now less than 1 percent. In the 1960s, the audit rate had been over 5 percent, but it has been declining ever since, a casualty of the agency's rising caseload and the growing complexity of many tax cases. Corporate audit rates have dropped even more than individual audit rates, falling from 14 percent in 1964 to about 2 percent in 1989.

Feast and Famine

Though the IRS was in the uncommon position among domestic federal agencies of having both its budget and staff increase significantly during the 1980s, agency officials have pointed to the budget process as a reason for its current problems.

IRS Commissioner Fred T. Goldberg, Jr. has described Congress's allotment of budget and personnel to the agency as "feast or famine," as the agency's budget increases fluctuated during the 1980s, from a high of 14 percent in 1987 to a low for fiscal 1990 of less than 3 percent.

Staffing levels. The same was true of staffing levels. Goldberg explains: "Yes, the IRS has experienced staffing growth over the decade, but it wasn't planned growth. . . . It was thousands of people one year, followed by a hiring freeze the next. It was classic mismanagement. . . . The system wasn't working." For example, a hiring freeze that lasted for all of fiscal 1990 left the examination division's technical staff smaller than it was two years earlier. Goldberg further contends, "In many ways, we haven't grown at all."

Work loads. Meanwhile, work loads at the IRS have grown, exacerbating existing problems. Between 1981 and 1990, the number of tax returns filed increased from 160 million to 190 million, and the number of filed tax documents doubled, from 600 million to 1.2 billion. Continual changes to many of the 2,381 sections of the tax code required dozens of new forms—as well as changes to existing forms and computer and training programs. New mandates to go after money laundering, to track culprits in the savings and loan scandal, and to enlist in the national war on drugs have siphoned off much of IRS's increases in staff, thus swamping the people charged with carrying out other agency functions.

Problems with People

Goldberg states that more people and funds would help boost audit rates and cut IRS accounts receivable—the type of comment most agency administrators are apt to make. However, the erratic resource allocations of the 1980s has made the IRS wary of bringing in too much staff all at one time. For example, the productivity of agency veterans declines whenever there are new personnel to be trained, which cuts the amount of revenue the agency collects.

Growth, moreover, won't produce the kind of revenue Congress once counted on when it boosted the IRS's enforcement budget to its current level of $3.5 billion. Back in 1986, the Congressional Budget Office projected that each additional dollar spent on enforcement would produce $16 in added revenues, but such gains appear to be no longer possible. In 1991, the IRS projected that a $191 million increase in enforcement spending will bring in $537 million that would otherwise go uncollected, less than a 3:1 ratio.

Quality of new personnel. Part of the problem with the agency's performance lies with the quality of incoming IRS employees. Low entry-level salaries and slow promotions dissuade many of the nation's best college graduates from accepting positions at the IRS. A largely ineffective college recruitment program, itself handicapped by erratic funding and the agency's decentralization, has also made it tougher to attract the best recruits.

Therefore, the IRS often winds up with mediocre recruits. For instance, between 1984 and 1987 the agency used a standardized exam developed by the American Institute of Certified Public Accountants to assess the performance of its new revenue officers. Their average was consistently in the 25th percentile or lower.

Retaining IRS employees is also a problem. Nearly 60 percent of the senior IRS executives are eligible to retire in 1992, and more than 60 percent of those eligible have indicated that they will leave within a year of their retirement date.

Agency personnel find themselves continually outgunned, particularly when dealing with corporate taxpayers. Sophisticated corporate cases, which can take five years or more to prepare and prosecute, are often beyond the abilities of all but the most experienced staffers. More than 80 percent of IRS tax dollar assessments on corporations are appealed, and more than 75 percent of the dollar amount in the contested assessment is overturned.

Computer Collapse

For all the other challenges facing the IRS, computers remain the agency's Achilles' heel. Machines designed with technology of the 1950s and installed in the early 1960s are still responsible for virtually all elements of the agency's revenue collection operations. In an age where on-line information is widely available to consumers instantly, it often takes the IRS several weeks to answer taxpayers' routine questions.

Antiquated computers slow down efficiency. For instance, bringing taxpayers' records to the computer screen when answering inquiries on the telephone is not yet possible at the IRS. Staff members can only send inquiries to the agency's central processing operations, in Martinsburg, West Virginia, where they are lined up with thousands of other similar requests. And, if the information the staff gets back is not relevant to the original inquiry, the process must begin all over again. Thus, for a public accustomed to the sophisticated marketing and customer service operations of such companies as American Express, the IRS's archaic computer system leaves the public with the impression that the agency is backward and inefficient. Indeed, it reinforces beliefs that federal workers can't—or won't—do their jobs.

A computer modernization program has been under way at IRS for 20 years, but its completion has been frustrated by high turnover among IRS executives responsible for the systems. Poor planning, a flinty Congress unwilling to spend the money, and federal procurement rules all have hampered the IRS's ability to update the computers critical to processing hundreds of millions of tax forms. The agency recently outlined its latest attempt to purchase modern computers, and has told

Congress that with the new machines it will process tomorrow's increased demands with today's work force. Perhaps this, the third modernization attempt, will be the charm.

CONSUMER PRODUCT SAFETY COMMISSION (CPSC)

Creation

The Consumer Product Safety Commission (CPSC), though created in 1974 by the signature of a Republican president, under Ronald Reagan quickly lost whatever power had been gained in the first seven years of its existence. Richard Nixon approved CPSC in another age, when the nation's regulatory agenda was reaching its peak, and when government's intervention in the economy to protect its citizens from personal harm seemed to be a legitimate item on the national agenda.

Decline of the CPSC.   The early promise of CPSC, that it would warn consumers of harmful products and that it would prevent such goods from remaining on the market, has never really been fulfilled. Indeed, this independent federal agency has spent most of its short history in decline.

Ronald Reagan came into office in January 1981 determined to get government off the back of America—and particularly off the back of American industry. Conservatives and industry leaders applauded as the new administration began to work its deregulatory will on the Environmental Protection Agency (EPA), the Federal Trade Commission (FTC), the Food and Drug Administration (FDA), the Occupational Safety and Health Administration (OSHA)—and the CPSC. Budgets were slashed; personnel cut. The CPSC has suffered more than its federal regulatory siblings during recent years, and even as the EPA and others have regained a portion of their former vigor under the Bush administration, the same cannot really be said for CPSC.

CPSC, a hollow agency.   If ever there was a hollow federal agency, CPSC is it. An estimated 22,500 Americans die each year, and another 3.4 million are injured, as a result of household accidents. Yet a severely handicapped CPSC is increasingly unable to help reduce that enormous toll. The number of products on store shelves grows ever more rapidly, but the ability of CPSC to review and assure that such goods are safe, or to inform the public when products are unsafe, deteriorates further with each passing year.

Shortage of funds delays investigations. A severe shortage of funds forces CPSC staff to delay investigations of product hazards and to spread investigations over several years. In some cases, CPSC's lack of resources means that the agency must totally ignore products which endanger Americans' safety. In dozens of instances, states have moved to regulate and recall questionable products within their borders because the federal regulators simply were not doing their job. Indeed, consumer advocates concluded in a 1990 study of CPSC that the agency's "limited budget has become an indirect culprit in the thousands of deaths and hundreds of thousands of injuries suffered each year by American consumers from unsafe products."[17]

Decline of an Agency

Few federal agencies have borne the brunt of deregulatory excess to the extent that CPSC has. It wasn't long into his administration before Reagan's politically and economically conservative appointees to the commission, people who looked askance at proactive federal intervention, were ignoring staff requests for budget increases and program expansions, and instead were recommending cuts in CPSC's budget and staff.

The CPSC has always been the smallest of the Washington's health- and safety-related regulatory agencies, even though its original mandate to protect the public against consumer product hazards has been expanded over the years to include enforcing the Federal Hazardous Substances Act, the Refrigerator Safety Act, the Poison Prevention Packaging Act, and the Flammable Fabrics Act.

Low budget causes CPSC to lose more ground. Its first year in business, CPSC had a $34 million budget, a funding level, which (in inflation-adjusted terms) essentially remained stable until 1981. During the eight years of the Reagan Administration, CPSC took a nose dive: Its $42.1 million fiscal 1981 budget fell to $34.5 million in fiscal 1989. Staff, in the same period, was cut from 978 to 519 employees. Still, the agency was required to oversee the safety of some 15,000 consumer products.

And even though its fiscal 1991 appropriation climbed to $35 million, the increase continues the agency's recent sad budget history—when adjusted for inflation, CPSC has been steadily losing ground. In preparing budgets for commissioners, in fact, CPSC staff estimates that taking only inflation into account since 1985, and not counting the added duties that Congress has heaped on the agency in its short history, CPSC's fiscal 1991 budget should have been $45.5 million, about $10 million more than the $35 million actually appropriated.[18]

Meanwhile, CPSC's short life has been filled with management problems and political gamesmanship. For nearly a decade the commission operated without a congressional reauthorization, and in the process failed to gain either the legislature's confidence or any more money. Conservatives in Congress, seeking to keep CPSC under tight rein, and liberals, unable to muster enough support for breathing new life into the agency, deadlocked for most of the 1980s.

Commission's political structure cause of ineffectiveness. Playing with the commission's political structure also has contributed to the agency's ineffectiveness. As part of the Reagan-era budget cuts, the number of commissioners at CPSC was cut from five to three, a move that staffers and consumer advocates regarded as a raw attempt by the Reagan administration to lower the agency's profile. Reducing the number of commissioners also gave any one commissioner the power to shut down the agency when disapproving of CPSC's activities, because three members were still required for quorums.

In fact, CPSC spent an unusual amount of time during the 1980s without a quorum, which meant that new projects and even such routine tasks as obtaining subpoenas, could not be undertaken. At such quorumless times, which on occasion lasted for nearly a year, CPSC's activity virtually ground to a halt.

Quality of commissioners inadequate. Moreover, the quality of CPSC's commissioners was not always what they might have been. At one point in the late 1980s, for instance, all the nominated or serving commissioners were under investigation by federal investigators or Congress for alleged financial or ethical violations, though no charges were filed or nominations rejected. And few of CPSC's commissioners had any experience in the consumer and health safety field. Like most political appointees of the era, they had Reagan campaign experience and conservative political credentials. Not surprising then that the commissioners often ignored the professional staff's recommendations on investigations and pretended that severe shortages in funds, equipment, and personnel did not exist.

Performance Problems

The vision of a proactive regulatory organization that could investigate and recall faulty products, and thereby save lives, has become in reality a reactive agency that too often waits for manufacturers to volunteer remedies to product problems or does not investigate until there's been unnecessary death or dismemberment.

All-terrain vehicles hazardous. For years, CPSC kept an eye on the mounting number of deaths and injuries occurring among the young riders of three-wheeled all-terrain vehicles (ATVs), but lacked the resources to investigate the hazard. When it decided to finally act on the problem in the late-1980s, the agency was forced to take funds and personnel from other CPSC investigations, some of which dealt with equally dangerous situations.

The agency's enforcement of ATV regulations has been hampered by conservative agendas which encouraged industry's voluntary cooperation with product standards. CPSC worked out an agreement with ATV manufacturers prohibiting the sale of the adult-size vehicles for use by children. The voluntary guidelines, however, have been flagrantly violated by some ATV distributors. Even after being chided by Congress, CPSC has done little to resolve the problem or enforce stricter standards. In fact, in fiscal 1991 the White House budget office eliminated funds to continue monitoring compliance of the agreement.

Moreover, even with the drastically reduced size of the agency technical staff responsible for evaluating product hazards, CPSC is given little money for private sector technical assistance. This makes it more difficult for CPSC to start new initiatives because the agency is unable to accurately assess products and their safety-related problems.

Consider the following examples in which CPSC has been unable to do its job:

- Budget constraints have forced CPSC to delay projects designed to improve the information available on poisonings or to evaluate the effectiveness of child-resistant packaging and safety caps on medicine bottles.
- Requests for funds to better communicate information on recalled products have been denied. CPSC also has been unable to secure funds to notify state and local governments about trends in product hazards or to collect information from them about emerging problems.
- Sometimes CPSC is unable to inform its own field staff about products that violate federal safety laws. The agency used to produce a regularly distributed memo to field offices that listed offending products, but it was discontinued in the mid-1980s. Field staffs, as a result, often have no way of knowing the status of product investigations or whether or not product recalls have been enforced. Without adequate information, field staff lack complete details about which products should not be on retailers' shelves. In the case of toys, the lack of this information is especially important, since 70 percent of 800 to 1,000 tested toys violate federal laws.[19]
- Budget cuts have eradicated staff to do legal and compliance enforcement work necessary to establish mandatory

industry standards. As a result, CPSC has deferred, either formally or informally, to at least 16 voluntary standards for products such as all-terrain vehicles, cribs, bunk beds, BB guns, and kerosene heaters. Yet budget cuts also have eliminated staff whose job it is to ensure that manufacturers are keeping their promises for safer products.

Funds to run agency lacking. The CPSC is replete with stories of hand-me-down equipment that barely works and of CPSC employees paying for supplies out of their own pockets. Travel funds, critical to an agency whose job it is to review and warn others about unsafe products, are regularly cut to keep program funds alive. Money for training and for conferences is virtually nonexistent. For lack of funds, the agency even was forced to terminate its membership in a conference that examined manufacturers' voluntary compliance standards, clearly a critical part of CPSC's mission.

Moreover, there is little investment in the basic infrastructure of the commission. CPSC, in its 1991 budget request to Congress, asked for no money for further installing its office automation system or an integrated computer network, equipment common throughout the federal government. It has been reported that laboratory work on measuring carbon monoxide and other gases emitted from kerosene heaters for an indoor air quality project was long delayed because there were no funds available for test equipment. Antiquated equipment being discarded by another government agency was finally acquired by CPSC, but it broke down so often that one agency engineer estimated that more money was spent fixing the machines than would have been necessary to purchase the equipment new.[20]

Scarce funds also have meant that managers at times must choose between fixing broken-down photocopying machines and allowing employees to take necessary business trips. In fact, the trips themselves are often partially paid for from employees' pockets, as flinty government travel allowances, compounded by CPSC austerity, come up short when it is time to pay for business trips to the field.

NATIONAL PARK SERVICE

Except perhaps for the IRS and the Social Security Administration, the National Park Service is the one federal agency Americans have the most frequent contact with in any given year. Created by Congress in 1916 to watch over monuments to nature and the nation's history, the park service is steward to 354 national parks, historic sites, and recreation areas throughout the country and its territories.

The park system is huge. Comprising about 80 million acres, since 1978 it has added some 60 parks and expanded by more than 49 million acres, more than doubling in size. Park rangers were hosting nearly 350 million people in the park system by 1990, about 100 million more people than actually live in the United States. And more are coming. The park service estimates that by the year 2010, half a billion people will visit the parks annually.

The National Park Service's Challenge

It is doubtful that the foresighted naturalists who fought to preserve the nation's extraordinary scenery and heritage a century ago ever imaged that so many people each year would validate their convictions about what ought to be treasured in America. Yet it is in the modern success of their vision that the park service today faces perhaps the greatest challenge of its stewardship of public lands. For as rangers attempt to preserve the parks unsullied for future generations, as Congress mandates, they also must cater to the growing demands of a recreation-seeking public, which, of course, Congress also mandates.

Demands on the park service continue to rise. In the past decade the number of park visitors increased by 25 percent, forcing the rangers to pay ever increasing attention to simply keeping order. Adding seven national parks in Alaska and dozens of others across the country have stretched thin the park service's limited supply of rangers even as stress on many of the most-visited parks, such as Yellowstone and Yosemite, threatens to destroy their uniqueness.

Park deterioration. The state of the parks has deteriorated, endangering the very purpose of their preservation. Development, logging, and mining encroach on park boundaries. Acid rain and air pollution harm the natural environment and block views. Human congestion has brought the urban problems of rising crime and stalled traffic to once pristine places. And an increase in the animal inhabitants searching for food and safety outside park boundaries worries wildlife biologists and says much about the parks' conditions.

The Reagan administration's emphasis on the lumber, mining, and cattle development of public lands adjacent to the parks has added to the deterioration of the park system. Reagan's prodevelopment philosophy, espoused by the now infamous Secretary of the Interior, James Watt, and his successor, Donald Hodel, also was responsible for a nearly decade-long moratorium on the purchase of new parkland. Under Reagan, private concessioners were encouraged to take on ever greater portions of the parks' recreation and management, abetting more development within the parks themselves.

The Reagan administration's political appointees, such as Watt and other prodevelopment people brought into the Interior Department and the park service, cared little for the century-old legacy that many believed had wrongly shut out millions of choice acres for natural resource development; thus, when it came time to defend park service budgets and argue for additional resources to meet the rising demands, many were unwilling to serve as advocates for the parks' conservation.

Appointees' takeover threatens agency. Political appointees to the Department of the Interior had so much sway over the park service that Congress in the late 1980s threatened to make the agency independent from its cabinet department overseers. Park superintendents who disagreed with the new conservative philosophy were sometimes transferred from important parks and many veteran rangers, long willing to put up with some of the worst pay in government service for the opportunity to work amid natural settings, resigned. High-level career executives in the park service found themselves routinely cut off from major decisions. And when political appointees tried to further consolidate their hold over park service matters by transferring its policy development office to the Interior Department, the "reorganization" was reversed only after angry legislators threatened to withhold paychecks of the responsible officials.

Decline and Deterioration

Our national parks are now as much monuments to Hollow Government as they are preserves for historic and natural settings. For more than a decade as demands have risen, the park service has watched its maintenance backlog steadily rise, even as its staffing in many parks remained flat. Today, for example, the park service is behind about $2 billion in repairs and maintenance. Rangers and park supervisors have stood by virtually helpless as buildings literally have crumbled for lack of repairs, and they had no choice but to close roads and bridges, trails and toilets, to the public.

Famous landmarks and buildings become disasters. The deterioration of the parks is not limited to buildings or public restrooms in some remote corner of the country; it afflicts the most popular and important parts of the national system. Among the most notable disasters is Independence National Historic Park in Philadelphia, the home of American icons such as the Liberty Bell and Independence Hall, the place where the Constitution and the Declaration of Independence were signed. Despite the ever rising number of visitors, the park's budget remained static for most of the 1980s, while its staff was cut by nearly one-third.[21]

For the past decade, the park service has not had sufficient funds to keep the buildings at the historic park in good repair, the most dramatic result of which has been water leaking from the roof onto the floor of Independence Hall. By 1990, more than one-third of the historic buildings in the park, including the Second Bank of the United States, the first home of the U.S. Supreme Court, and the house where Thomas Jefferson drafted the Declaration of Independence, had been closed.

One full block of Independence Mall had been barricaded because funds were unavailable to fix broken sidewalks, busted lampposts, and rotting benches. The park superintendent warned that other buildings, including Congress Hall, where part of the Bill of Rights had been written, might be shuttered as well.[22]

And if operations and maintenance are this bad at the cradle of democracy, visited by some 600,000 people annually, they are even worse elsewhere. Consider the following examples where demands have clearly overwhelmed investment:

- Hundreds of miles of hiking trails, from Arcadia National Park in Maine to Olympic National Park in Washington, remain closed for lack of funds to maintain them or spare rangers available to do maintenance work.

- After fires raged through Yellowstone National Park, causing considerable damage to the property and the park service's image, the agency and its sister, the U.S. Forest Service, still lack enough equipment, staff, and training resources required to prevent another disaster such as the 1988 inferno.

- Park service employees are spread so thin at many national sites as to be almost nonexistent. Although this situation exists in many of the large parks in the continental United States, it is even more prevelant in the vast system of Alaska parks and refuges created by Congress in 1978. For instance, the 19.4 million-acre Arctic National Wildlife Refuge, often called "America's Serengeti" for its abundance and variety of wildlife, has just 1.3 park service employees for every 1 million acres of refuge land. At Denali National Park, the home of Mount McKinley, the highest peak in North America, the park service can afford to employ just two backcountry rangers to supervise more than 6 million acres. Funds for Denali have remained essentially flat since the mid-1980s, while at the same time the number of visitors has more than doubled.[23]

- Funds for resource management and research at many national parks are well below what is required to obtain even a basic understanding of the plants and animals within their boundaries, undermining attempts to better manage and protect wildlife for the future. Research represents just 2 percent of the park service's budget.

• Crime continues to grow at national parks, where rangers now must carry firearms, handcuffs, and nightsticks—and some even wear bulletproof vests. In 1990, more than $500 million worth of illegal drugs were seized in the parks. The rangers' jobs have become so similar to a policeman's that they have petitioned Congress to reclassify their work as law enforcement. As a result, a ranger's traditional job of interpreting the natural and historic scenery to visitors has largely been handed over to park volunteers. The forced change in job description, combined with woeful starting salaries, has made it increasingly difficult for the park service to recruit young rangers.

Congress and the Parks

Of course, Congress loves the National Park Service. Parks are powerful economic tools for local development, representing both new jobs for the rural communities in which most parks are situated, and a flood of tourist dollars.

Legislators add parks for constituents. Thus, legislators, ever vigilant for opportunities to bring home to constituents federal largesse, have become increasingly adept at creating new parks and monuments. At first glance, such regard for nature or history among politicians seems laudable. But in reality, many new parks are barely disguised pork barrel projects that have little national significance and serve mainly to siphon off scarce park service resources from more pressing needs.

Indeed, Park Service Director James M. Ridenour was so concerned about the trend of legislators to create ad hoc parks that he recently wrote in the agency's magazine: "We are spreading our limited resources over a growing base and . . . we may suffer the possibility of sliding into mediocrity."[24]

Federal deficit grows in park system. To be sure, the Democratic Congress created new parks through much of the 1980s because the Reagan administration was more interested in limiting the system's expansion. And the park service, eager to have certain parcels of land known for their historic or natural significance added to the system, was happy to go along.

Yet as the growing federal deficit in the past few years has begun limiting the money that legislators can funnel back home, many have taken more creative tacks, including the creation of national parks of dubious merit within their district. Often these parks are added to appropriations bills at the last minute, making it impossible for the park service, other legislators, or the public, to review and comment on the proposals.

In fiscal 1991, for instance, over the objection of park service officials, Congress earmarked millions of dollars for dozens of projects and acquisitions that have little to do with the agency's traditional mission. When tallied up, Congress appropriated $271 million in new construction funds for the park service, more than three times the agency's or the administration's request. One boondoggle, a monument to entertainer Lawrence Welk, became so infamous as an example of pork barrel politics, that Congress later took the uncommon step of taking the new park off the construction list.

Unfortunately, at the same time that the park service is $2 billion behind in urgently needed repairs and maintenance and forced to forgo more than $200 million in natural resource projects for lack of funds, Congress is telling it to tackle an industrial theme park in Pennsylvania pushed by Rep. John Murtha (D, Pa.), a powerful congressman; a new visitors' center at Fort Larned National Historic Site in Larned, Kansas, insisted upon by Senate Minority Leader Robert Dole (R, Kan.), even after the park service had decided that the existing center was adequate; and the $4.5 million renovation of a supposedly historic moviehouse at the behest of arguably the Senate's ablest pork barreler, Robert Byrd (D, W.Va.).

No doubt each of these will find its place alongside Yellowstone and Yosemite as crown jewels of the National Park System. In the meantime, the "National Pork Service," as some staffers have come to call the agency, will continue to spread its quickly thinning resources throughout an ever growing number of legitimate—and absurd—demands.

Epilogue

I n the months after the Berlin Wall came tumbling down, many Americans looked with pride and fascination upon the fledgling democracies of Eastern Europe. In a February 1990 address to a joint session of the U.S. Congress, Vaclav Havel, the playwright-president of a free Czechoslovakia, spoke reverently about "the simple and important act of human spirit" embodied in the Declaration of Independence and its impact on those who sought freedom. Indeed, America had been a beacon of hope piercing more than four gray decades of Communism and state control.

THE PEACE CORPS

George Bush reveled in Communism's failure and used the opportunity to make, through his self-proclaimed fondness for foreign policy, a gesture supporting the new democracies. The president dispatched the Peace Corps, plebian ambassadors to third-world countries, to Eastern Europe. They were to teach English to the Iron Curtain's citizens, helping to open these shuttered nations to the West's economic and political landscape.

It was a noble gesture, but here Kennedy's vision came face to face with Reagan's republic. In turning to the Peace Corps to be America's representative, Bush unwittingly sent forth a symbol of the Hollow Government.

Those who looked closely at the American hand outstretched across the ocean would have detected a bit of palsey. In the 1990s, the Peace Corps attracts barely one-fifth of the volunteer applications that it received in 1964; furthermore, the corps is unable to fill 40 percent of its scientific and technical positions or to attract significant numbers of minorities. Nearly one-third quit before their tour of duty ends. Overall, the agency has been weakened dramatically in the past 20 years by budget cuts and by a lack of commitment from Kennedy's successors in the Oval Office.[1]

Perhaps the Peace Corps will serve as a warning to Eastern Europe. For the new democracies can still avoid what the United States could not. Deficit spending, political parochialism, and disregard for public service are not uniquely American flaws, but the mistakes made in this country can still be minimized in other nations.

HOPEFUL CHANGES IN WASHINGTON

Meanwhile, there have been some hopeful notes of change in Washington. To its credit, the Bush administration has made marginal improvements designed to correct the staffing and budgetary blight of the Reagan antigovernment era. Many federal agencies today are more capable of carrying out their enforcement and service delivery missions than at any time in the past decade. Enforcement staffs have been strengthened at the Environmental Protection Agency (EPA) and at the independent regulatory commissions, including the Food and Drug Administration and the Federal Trade Commission. The Consumer Product Safety Commission finally was reauthorized in 1990 after almost a decade of neglect and provided with additional resources.

Attention also is being paid to correct deficiencies in those cabinet departments where waste, fraud, and abuse seem most prevelant. For instance, Office of Management and Budget-orchestrated teams have helped improve management practices and prevent future losses at the Farmers Home Administration, the Bureau of Indian Affairs, and in the student financial aid programs of the Department of Education.

Overhaul of Civil Service Pay System

Moreover, the White House supported both a much-needed overhaul of the civil service pay system and the creation of executive branch chief financial officers, who will work to shore up the government's shoddy accounting and budget systems. The OMB has added staff to its management side, reversing a gradual 20-year decline in its ability to contend with governmentwide problems. Morale in the civil service appears higher than it has in years. Also, there are early indications that the image of public service is improving among college students making career decisions—although the public sector's job stability during the recession undoubtedly has been a factor.

Congress Matures

Even Congress has shown signs of maturity. The Budget Enforcement Act of 1990, for all of its faults, could lead to a budget surplus in the late 1990s, which in turn could allow domestic discretionary spending to stop shrinking. And legislators have become moderately more attuned to the work loads of federal agencies and now will often provide additional staff and budget authority when assigning new responsibilities. The EPA received additional hiring authority to implement the Clean Air Act of 1990, and the Justice Department, belatedly, was allowed to hire more attorneys and investigators to combat financial fraud in the banking industry.

THE HOLLOW GOVERNMENT CONTINUES

These changes, however welcome, are dwarfed by problems inherent in an organization with a $1.52 trillion budget and more than $399 billion deficit. The government still is—and for the forseeable future, will be—hollow. Even with more staff and higher budgets, domestic agencies, the lucky ones, are only now approaching operating levels that they had attained before the Reagan-era cuts.

National Population Increases

Since 1980, meanwhile, the nation's population has grown almost 10 percent (the executive branch has increased by 0.8 percent in the same period), inflation has climbed more than 60 percent (as the domestic discretionary budget fell), and the gross national product has expanded by nearly $2.8 trillion. Quite simply, the federal government in many instances is facing the problems of the 1990s with late 1970s resources.

And no one should expect any significant change. New funds to fill in the Hollow Government, where they exist, will be used for election-inspired tax breaks and nagging problems of a neglected past such as the banking industry's collapse and the cleanup of government's monumental hazardous waste dumps. Furthermore, the biggest impact on federal spending is yet to come, as the entitlement bills for the Baby Boomers' retirement and health care begin showing up.

Federal Medicare Costs

Between now and 1995, for instance, government's outlays for mandatory spending will grow by more than $200 million each month. Federal Medicare costs have roughly doubled every five years since 1975 and will total about $95 billion by 1995. Just after 2000, in fact, spending on Medicare will exceed costs for Social Security or the nation's defense. And that's not including increased demands to help the 34 million Americans without health care or to provide financing for a national health care system. Even current law obligations are not fully covered by projected future receipts, and already account for more than $250 billion in unfunded liabilities just for Medicare hospital insurance.

Other programs are growing at an equally alarming rate. Entitlements could account for nearly 60 percent of the federal budget by 1995, up from less than 25 percent when Kennedy was president. Some of the future's big ticket items are worth mentioning here.

Benefits for Federal Employees

Mandatory outlays for federal employees' health benefits will have more than doubled between 1991 and 1995, rising from $3.2 billion to $6.5 billion. Likewise, costs to support the 2.2 million retirees receiving pension benefits under the Civil Service Retirement System and other federal retirement plans also are straining the budget's seams. Costs will grow by more than one-third by the mid-1990s.

The Rail Pension Fund

The Federal Railroad Retirement Board, which pays benefits to 903,000 annuitants, could be bankrupt by 2013. Congress has shored up the retirement account six times since World War II—three times in the 1980s. Since 1983, Congress had given the rail pension fund more than $3 billion in direct subsidies. Because the private rail industry has consistently overestimated employment projections, which in turn influence pension fund balances, significant cash flow shortages have plagued the system. In 1990, the fund had a reported actuarial deficiency of some $14 billion.

Social Security

Then there is Social Security. Driven by demographics, as are the other mandatory programs, the retirement of the Baby-Boom generation will literally bust the Social Security system. A short-term fix in the early 1980s avoided impending bankruptcy then, but demand from the Old Age Survivors and Disability Insurance trust funds will exceed income beginning in 2017 and, without reform, will deplete reserves by about 2043.

HOPE FOR THE FUTURE

No doubt each of these and other unforeseen financial disasters will be resolved, if history is any guide, as they reach the crisis point. The bills coming due will divert scarce resources from future investment to current consumption. This will further fuel a deficit that future generations will be forced to pay. Indeed, the quality of life for our children and grandchildren, and the state of their government, are bound to suffer. Hollow Government will get worse unless today's politicians collect the courage necessary to realign priorities, and restrain the time-honored provision of programs and services that assured their reelection.

Though more than 200 years old, democracy in America is still evolving. We embrace the process, but still resent the product. For this to change, for Americans to respect and participate in true democracy, first requires those who are elected as leaders to pay more attention to the management of government and the country than they do their own careers. Only then will public service regain the people's trust.

Endnotes

Introduction

1. *Public Papers of the Presidents: Dwight David Eisenhower 1961* (Washington, D.C.: U.S. Government Printing Office, 1961), p. 410.

2. Anonymous, "If Kennedy Wins White House—Look for the 'Young Deal,'" *U.S. News and World Report* 49, no. 4 (July 25, 1960), p. 54.

3. Ibid.

4. *Public Papers of the Presidents: John F. Kennedy 1961* (Washington, D.C.: U.S. Government Printing Office, 1961), pp. 1–2.

5. David Halberstam, *The Best and the Brightest* (New York: Random House, 1969), p. 41.

6. *Public Papers of the Presidents: Richard Nixon 1969* (Washington, D.C.: U.S. Government Printing Office, 1971), p. 2.

7. U.S. Senate, *Senate Select Committee on Presidential Campaign Activities* (Washington, D.C.: U.S. Government Printing Office, June–July 1973), Book 6, p. 2518.

8. *Public Papers of the Presidents: Richard Nixon 1973* (Washington, D.C.: U.S. Government Printing Office, 1975), p. 2.

9. Richard P. Nathan, *The Plot that Failed: Nixon and the Administrative Presidency* (New York: John Wiley & Sons, 1975), p. 49.

10. Harold Seidman and Robert Gilmour, *Politics, Position and Power* (New York: Oxford University Press, 1986), pp. 102–3.

11. Jimmy Carter, *Keeping Faith* (New York: Bantam Books, 1982), p. 127.

12. *Public Papers Nixon 1973; and Public Papers of the Presidents: Jimmy Carter 1977*, Volume 1 (Washington, D.C.: U.S. Government Printing Office, 1977), pp. 14 and 2, respectively.

13. Jimmy Carter quoted in John R. Dempsey, "Carter Reorganization: A Midterm Appraisal," *Public Administration Review* 39, no. 1 (January–February 1979), p. 74.

14. *Public Papers of the Presidents: Jimmy Carter 1979* (Washington, D.C.: U.S. Government Printing Office, 1980), p. 105.

15. Seidman and Gilmour, *Politics, Position and Power*, p. 113.

16. David Stockman, *The Triumph of Politics* (New York: Avon Books, 1986), p. 9.

17. *Public Papers of the Presidents: Ronald Reagan 1981* (Washington, D.C.: U.S. Government Printing Office, 1982), p. 2.

18. Ibid.

19. Ibid., p. 5.

Chapter One

1. As reported in *SSA's First Lady: Ida May Fuller* (Washington, D.C.: Historian's Office, Social Security Administration, 1990), p. 1.

2. Ibid.

3. 1991 Advisory Council on Social Security, *Interim Report on Social Security and the Federal Budget* (Washington, D.C., July 1990), p. 4.

4. Sylvester J. Schieber, *Social Security: Perspectives on Preserving the System* (Washington, D.C.: Employee Benefit Research Institute, 1982), p. 19.

5. 1991 Advisory Council, *Interim Report*, p. 4.

6. Executive Office of the President, *Budget of the United States Government, Fiscal Year 1992* (Washington, D.C.: U.S. Government Printing Office, 1991), Part One, p. 13.

7. Richard B. Morris, *Encyclopedia of American History* (New York: Harper & Row, 1965), p. 529.

8. Ibid, p. 530.

9. Carolyn Webber and Aaron Wildavsky, *A History of Taxation and Expenditure in the Western World* (New York: Simon & Schuster, 1986), p. 384.

10. Ibid.

11. Ibid.

12. Arthur M. Schlesinger Jr., *The Coming of the New Deal* (Boston: Houghton Mifflin, 1959), p. 315.

13. Executive Office, *Budget . . ., Fiscal Year 1992*, Part Seven, p. 106.

14. As reported in Frank Levy, *Dollars and Dreams: The Changing American Income Distribution* (New York: Russell Sage Foundation, 1987), p. 37.

15. Executive Office of the President, *Budget of the United States Government, Fiscal Year 1990 Historical Tables* (Washington, D.C.: U.S. Government Printing Office, 1990), p. 188.

16. James L. Sundquist, *Politics and Policy: The Eisenhower, Kennedy and Johnson Years* (Washington, D.C.: The Brookings Institution, 1968), p. 113.

17. *Public Papers of the Presidents: Lyndon Baines Johnson 1964* (Washington, D.C.: U.S. Government Printing Office, 1965), p. 114.

18. Sheldon Danziger and Robert Plotnick, "The War on Income Poverty: Achievements and Failures," in Paul M. Sommers, ed., *Welfare Reform in America: Perspectives and Prospects* (Boston: Kluwer-Nijhoff Publishing, 1982), p. 34.

19. Executive Office, *Budget . . . , Fiscal Year 1992*, Part Seven, p. 105.

20. Martin Anderson, *Welfare* (Stanford, Calif.: Hoover Institution Press, 1978), p. 4.

21. Ibid., p. 7.

22. Executive Office, *Budget . . ., Fiscal Year 1992*, Part Seven, p. 105.

23. Advisory Commission on Intergovernmental Relations, *Significant Features of Fiscal Federalism, 1988 Edition* (Washington, D.C., 1987), p. 15.

24. U.S. Department of Health and Human Services, Administration for Children, Youth and Families, *Project Head Start Statistical Fact Sheet* (Washington, D.C., January 1991).

25. U.S. Department of Agriculture, Food and Nutrition Service, Annual Historical Records (Washington, D.C., 1990).

26. U.S. Department of Labor, Employment and Training Administration, database statistics from the Office of Trade Adjustment Assistance (Washington, D.C., 1990).

27. U.S. Department of Health and Human Services, Health Care Financing Administration, *1990 HCFA Statistics* (Washington, D.C., September 1990), pp. 6, 25.

28. Congressional Budget Office, *The Economic and Budget Outlook: Fiscal Years 1992–1996* (Washington, D.C.: U.S. Government Printing Office, January 1991), p. 151.

29. Dan Morgan, "In College of 'Cardinals' a Summer of Frustration," *The Washington Post*, June 30, 1989, A14.

30. Ibid.

31. Congressional Budget Office, *Trends in Public Investment* (Washington, D.C., 1987), p. xiii.

32. U.S. General Accounting Office, *FAA Staffing, Better Strategy Needed to Ensure Facilities Are Properly Staffed*, GAO/RCED-92-8 (Washington, D.C., October 16, 1991), p. 3.

33. U.S. General Accounting Office, *Resource Limitations Affect Condition of Forest Service Recreation Sites*, GAO/RCED-91-48 (Washington, D.C., January 1991), p. 2.

34. Congressional Budget Office, *Reforming Federal Deposit Insurance* (Washington, D.C., September 1990), p. 14.

35. Executive Office, *Budget . . . , Fiscal Year 1992*, Part Two, p. 202.

36. Ibid.

37. Ibid.

38. Congressional Budget Office, *Controlling the Risks of Government-Sponsored Enterprises* (Washington, D.C., April 1991), p. 7.

39. U.S. General Accounting Office, *Government-Sponsored Enterprises: The Government's Exposure to Risk* (Washington, D.C., August 1990), p. 27.

Chapter Two

1. As quoted in "A Proposition Taxpayers Couldn't Refuse," *Time* 113, no. 1 (January 1, 1979), p. 41.

2. "Sound and Fury over Taxes," *Time* 111, no. 25 (June 19, 1978), p. 13.

3. "A Proposition . . . , *Time*, p. 41.

4. Ibid.

5. Karlyn H. Keene and Everett C. Ladd, "Government As Villain: Has the Era Ended?" *Government Executive* 20, no. 1 (January 1988), p. 13.

6. Ibid., pp. 13–14.

7. As quoted in William Schneider, "The Political Legacy of the Reagan Years," in Sidney Blumenthal and Thomas Byrne Edsall, *The Reagan Legacy* (New York: Pantheon Books, 1988), pp. 74–75.

8. Anonymous, "Opinion Outlook," *The National Journal* 21, no. 6 (April 22, 1989), p. 1015.

9. Herbert Stein, *Presidential Economics* (Washington, D.C.: American Enterprise Institute, 1988), p. 107.

10. Ibid., pp. 110–12.

11. Walter W. Heller, "Supply-Side Follies of 1981," *The Wall Street Journal*, June 12, 1981, p. 20.

12. As quoted in Robert W. Merry and Kenneth H. Bacon, "Supply-Side Economics and How It Grew from a Theory to a Presidential Program," *The Wall Street Journal*, February 18, 1981, p. 48.

13. As quoted in Pamela Fessler, "Reagan Tax Plan Ready for Economic Test," *Congressional Quarterly* 39, no. 32 (August 8, 1981), p. 1431.

14. "Interview with Arthur B. Laffer, Economist, What Went Wrong with 'Supply Side' Economics," *U.S. News & World Report* 92, no. 2 (January 18, 1982), p. 36.

15. Executive Office of the President, *Budget of the United States Government, Fiscal Year 1992* (Washington, D.C.: U.S. Government Printing Office, 1991), Part Seven, p. 23.

16. William Niskanen, *Reaganomics* (New York: Oxford University Press, 1988), p. 76.

17. Lawrence J. Korb, "The 1991 Defense Budget," in Henry J. Aaron, ed., *Setting National Priorities* (Washington, D.C.: The Brookings Institution, 1990), p. 119.

18. Ibid.

19. Executive Office, *Budget . . . , Fiscal Year 1992*, Part Seven, p. 69.

20. Korb, in *Setting National Priorities*, p. 120.

21. Executive Office, *Budget . . . , Fiscal Year 1992*, Part Seven, P. 69–70.

22. Congressional Budget Office, *An Analysis of the President's Budgetary Proposals for Fiscal Year 1991* (Washington, D.C., March 1990), p. 70.

23. Jacques S. Gansler, *Affording Defense* (Cambridge, Mass.: The MIT Press, 1989), p. 7. Gansler's estimates come from his own work, as discussed in Chapter 6 of *Affording Defense*, as well as his previous book, *The Defense Industry* (Cambridge, Mass.: The MIT Press, 1980), and the final report of the Defense Systems Acquisition Review Council Working Group, 1972.

24. J. Ronald Fox, "Revamping the Business of National Defense," *Harvard Business Review* 62, no. 5 (September–October 1985), p. 63.

25. Jacques S. Gansler, "How to Improve the Acquisition of Weapons," in Robert J. Art et al., eds., *Reorganizing America's Defense* (Washington, D.C.: Pergamon-Brasseys, 1985), p. 384.

26. Mark Rovner, *Defense Dollars and Sense* (Washington, D.C.: Common Cause, 1983), p. 42.

27. OMB Watch, *The OMB Watcher* 8, no. 4 (September 30, 1990), p. 11.

28. Ibid.

29. Neil A. Lewis, "Regulatory Review Office in Dispute," *The New York Times*, May 5, 1990, p. 9.

30. OMB Watch, *The OMB Watcher*, p. 11.

31. U.S. General Accounting Office, *Revenues: Shortcomings in Onshore Federal Oil and Gas Production Verification*, GAO/RCED-90-99 (Washington, D.C., June 1990), pp. 3, 10.

32. *Anonymous*, "Contaminated Chickens," *The Washington Post*, May 27, 1991, p. A7.

33. Gene Bruce, "Dirty Chicken," *The Atlantic Monthly* 266, no. 5 (November 1990), p. 32.

34. U.S. Department of Health and Human Services, Advisory Committee on the Food and Drug Administration, *Final Report* (Washington, D.C., May 1991), p. 26.

35. U.S. General Accounting Office, *Occupational Safety & Health: Options for Improving Safety and Health in the Workplace*, GAO/HRD 90-66BR (Washington, D.C., August 1990), p. 59

36. Figures based on historical tables, Executive Office of the President, *Budget . . . , Fiscal Year 1992* (Washington, D.C.: U.S. Government Printing Office, 1991).

37. U.S. Office of Personnel Management, *The Federal Workforce* (Washington, D.C., May 1989).

38. As quoted in Mark L. Goldstein, "Hollow Government," *Government Executive* 21, no. 10 (October 1989) p. 16.

Chapter Three

1. Dana Priest, "Volunteers Collect Trash Piling Up in Shutdown," *The Washington Post*, October 9, 1990, p. A8.

2. James Sundquist, "Needed: A Political Theory for the New Era of Coalition Government in the United States," *Political Science Quarterly*, Winter 1988–1989, p. 629.

3. Aaron Wildavsky, *The New Politics of the Budgetary Process* (Glenview, Ill.: Scott Foresman, 1988), p. 236.

4. Norman J. Ornstein, Thomas E. Mann, and Michael J. Malbin, *Vital Statistics on Congress 1989–1990* (Washington, D.C.: Congressional Quarterly Inc., 1990), p. 117.

5. Mark L. Goldstein, "Our Myopic Legislature," *Government Executive* 23, no. 1 (January 1991), p. 13.

6. Karen Forestel, "Staff Turnover Rises Sharply with Half of All House Aides in Jobs Year or Less," *Roll Call*, October 22, 1990, p. 1.

7. Secretary of Defense, *White Paper on the Department of Defense and the Congress: Report to the President* (Washington, D.C., January 1990), p. 29.

8. Ornstein et al., *Vital Statistics*, p. 132.

9. Secretary of Defense, *White Paper*, p. 15.

10. Ibid, p. 10.

11. Energy and Environment Study Institute, *Statutory Deadlines in Environmental Legislation: Necessary But Need Improvement*, reported in: National Academy of Public Administration, *Congressional Oversight of Regulatory Agencies: The Need to Strike a Balance and Focus on Performance* (Washington, D.C., 1985), p. 20.

12. Robert Pear, "U.S. Laws Delayed by Complex Rules and Partisanship," *The New York Times*, March 31, 1991, p. Al.

13. Michael Weisskopf, "EPA Falls Far Short in Enforcing Drinking Water Laws," *The Washington Post*, May 20, 1991, p. A1.

14. Anonymous, "Byrd's Billion-Dollar Delivery," *The Washington Post*, April 16, 1991, p. A17.

15. Michael Isikoff, "Drug Center Arrives in Pork Barrel," *The Washington Post*, October 29, 1990, p. A13.

16. Kitty Dumas, "Secret Service Gets the Jump on S&L Bailout Crackdown," *Congressional Quarterly* 48, no. 28 (July 14, 1990), p. 2218.

17. Alissa J. Rubin, "Super Collider Surges Ahead Despite Concerns over Cost," *Congressional Quarterly* 49, no. 14 (April 6, 1991), p. 856.

Chapter Four

1. The National Commission on the Public Service, *Leadership for America: Rebuilding the Public Service* (Washington, D.C., 1989), p. 2.

2. Tom Shoop, "Combing the Campuses," *Government Executive* 23, no. 4 (April 1991), p. 22.

3. Ibid., p. 28.

4. Ibid., p. 29.

5. National Commission, *Leadership for America*, p. 26.

6. The Hudson Institute, *Civil Service 2000: Research Report for the U.S. Office of Personnel Management* (Washington, D.C.: U.S. Government Printing Office, 1988), p. 30.

7. National Commission, *Leadership for America*, p. 26.

8. U.S. General Accounting Office, *Federal Recruiting and Hiring: Making Government Jobs Attractive to Prospective Employees*, GAO/GGD-90-105 (Washington, D.C., August 1990), p. 20.

9. Ibid., p. 31.

10. Mark L. Goldstein, "Happy Birthday, SES?" *Government Executive* 21, no. 7 (July 1989), p. 12.

11. U.S. Merit Systems Protection Board, *Working for America: A Federal Employee Survey* (Washington, D.C.) 1990, p. 7.

12. Ibid., p. 8.

13. U.S. General Accounting Office, *Recruitment and Retention: Inadequate Federal Pay Cited as Primary Problem by Agency Officials*, GAO/GGD-90-117 (September 1990), p. 61.

14. Ibid., p. 63.

15. Ibid., p. 64.

16. Hudson Institute, *Civil Service 2000*, p. 6.

17. Ibid., p. 7.

18. U.S. Merit Systems Protection Board, *Who Is Leaving the Federal Government? An Analysis of Employee Turnover* (Washington, D.C., 1989), p. 2.

19. The National Commission on the Public Service, *Task Force Reports to the National Commission on the Public Service* (Washington, D.C., 1989), p. 84.

20. U.S. MSPB, *Who Is Leaving the Federal Government?* p. 13.

21. Anonymous, "Survey Finds Morale Rock Bottom," *Federal Employees' News Digest*, April 1989.

22. George Millburn, untitled speech, *Conference on Federal Workforce Quality Assessment*, sponsored by the Office of Personnel Management and U.S. Merit Systems Protection Board (Washington, D.C., May 8, 1989).

23. U.S. MSPB, *Working for America*, p. 11.

24. National Commission on the Public Service, *Task Force Reports*, p. 87.

25. Advisory Committee on Federal Pay, *Annual Report* (Washington, D.C., 1990), p. 1.

26. U.S. GAO, *Recruitment and Retention*, p. 61.

27. Office of Technology Assessment, *Assessing Contractor Use in Superfund* (Washington, D.C., January 1989), p. 32.

28. U.S. GAO, *Recruitment and Retention*, p. 62.

29. National Academy of Public Adminstration, *Recruiting Presidential Appointees: A Conference of Former Presidential Personnel Assistants* (Washington, D.C., 1984), p. 19.

30. Ibid., p. 10.

31. G. Calvin Mackenzie, "Appointing Mr. (or Ms.) Right," *Government Executive* 22, no. 4 (April 1990), p. 30.

32. As reported in the National Commission on the Public Service, *Task Force Reports*, p. 168.

33. U.S. Merit Systems Protection Board, *The Senior Executive Service: Views of Former Federal Executives* (Washington, D.C., 1989), p. 20.

34. Ibid., p. 21.

35. Ibid.

36. Joel D. Aberbach and Bert A. Rockman, "What Has Happened to the U.S. Senior Civil Service?" *The Brookings Review* 8, no. 4 (Fall 1990), p. 37.

Chapter Five

1. Morton J. Schussheim, *The Missions and Management of HUD: CRS Report for Congress,* Congressional Research Service (Washington, D.C., August 16, 1990), p. 6.

2. Molly Moore, "Sky-High Prices on Defense Items Circling Again," *The Washington Post,* July 13, 1990, p. A19.

3. Kathy Sawyer, "NASA Again Will Review Flaw-Detection System," *The Washington Post,* May 24, 1991, p. A3

4. U.S. General Accounting Office, *Program Evaluation Issues,* Transition Series, GAO/OCG-89-8TR (Washington, D.C., November 1988), p. 19.

5. Ibid., p. 7.

6. Office of the Inspector General, U.S. Department of the Interior, *Audit Report: Bureau of Land Management Forestry Operations in Western Oregon,* Report No. 90–105 (Washington, D.C., September 1990), p. 4.

7. U.S. General Accounting Office, *Improvements Needed in Procedures to Assure Physicians Are Qualified,* GAO/HRD-89-77 (Washington, D.C., August 1989), p. 2.

8. Molly Moore, "Memo Accuses Air Force of Ignoring B-2 Costs," *The Washington Post,* July 19, 1990, A14.

9. Anonymous, "Barred Firm Supplied Navy, Panel Reports," *The Washington Post,* July 16, 1991, A4.

10. Leonard D. White, *The Federalists* (New York: Macmillian, 1956), p. 123.

11. Ann Mariano, "FHA Losses Are Mounting, GAO Reports," *The Washington Post,* May 18, 1991, p. C1.

12. Executive Office of the President, *Budget of the United States Government, Fiscal Year 1992* (Washington, D.C.: U.S. Government Printing Office, 1991), Part Two, p. 331.

13. Ibid., p. 321.

14. Ibid., p. 331.

15. Keith Schneider, "Inquiry Says Indian Agency Loses Track of $95 Million," *The New York Times,* January 12, 1991, p. A11.

16. "Federal Internal Control and Financial Management Systems Remain Weak and Obsolete," Statement of Charles A. Bowsher, Comptroller General of the United States to the Committee on Governmental Affairs, United States Senate, November 29, 1989, p. 3.

17. Executive Office, *Budget . . . , Fiscal Year 1992,* Part Two, p. 317.

18. U.S. Senate, HUD/Mod Rehab Investigation Subcommittee of the Committee on Banking, Housing and Urban Affairs, *Final Report and Recom-*

mendations (Washington, D.C.: U.S. Government Printing Office, 1990), p. 148.

19. U.S. General Accounting Office, *Recruitment and Retention: Inadequate Federal Pay Cited as Primary Problem by Agency Officials*, GAO/GGD-90-117 (Washington, D.C., September 1990), p. 25.

20. U.S. General Accounting Office, *Federal Building: Actions Needed to Prevent Further Deterioration and Obsolescence*, GAO/GGD-91-57 (Washington, D.C., May 1991), p. 3.

21. Ibid.

22. Ibid., pp. 4, 28.

23. U.S. General Accounting Office, *NASA Maintenance: Stronger Commitment Needed to Curb Facility Deterioration*, GAO/NSIAD-91-34 (Washington, D.C., December 1990), p. 3.

24. U.S. GAO, *Federal Buildings*, p. 23.

25. Advisory Committee on the Food and Drug Administration, U.S. Department of Health and Human Services, *Final Report* (Washington, D.C., May 1991), p. 39.

26. Ibid., p. C-13.

27. As quoted in Sara Solberg and Jan Mason, "The Fragile Balance," *Life* 14, no. 6 (Summer Special 1991), p. 89.

28. U.S. General Accounting Office, *Information Resources: Management Commitment Needed to Meet Information Challenges*, GAO/IMTEC-90-27 (Washington, D.C., April 1990), p. 1.

29. Mark Goldstein, "Hollow Government," *Government Executive* 21, no. 10 (October 1989), p. 22.

30. U.S. General Accounting Office, *Problems Persist in Justice's ADP Management and Operations*, GAO/IMTEC-91-4 (Washington, D.C., November 1990), p. 8.

31. Noam Cohen, "Weather Service Faces Tough Test," *The New York Times*, January 13, 1991, p. A16.

32. Office of Inspector General, U.S. Department of Commerce, *Inspector General's Semiannual Report to the Congress* (Washington, D.C., November 1, 1990), p. 1.

Chapter Six

1. Statement of Admiral James D. Watkins, Secretary of Energy, before the Department of Energy Defense Nuclear Facilities Panel, U.S. House of Representatives (Washington, D.C., April 3, 1989), p. 2.

2. U.S. Senate Subcommittee on Federal Services, Post Office and Civil Service of the Committee on Governmental Affairs, "The Department of Energy's Reliance on Private Contractors to Perform the Work of Government," Report to the Chairman of the Federal Services Subcommittee by the Majority Staff (Washington, D.C., November 1989), pp. 19–20.

3. Executive Office of the President, *Special Analyses, Budget of the United States Government, Fiscal Year 1990* (Washington, D.C., 1989), p. 1–13.

4. Anonymous, "The Civil Service: A Statistical Profile," *Government Executive* 23, no. 4 (April 1991), p. 32.

5. Ibid., p. 29.

6. The term "Shadow Government" was first used by Daniel Guttman and Barry Willner in *The Shadow Government* (New York: Pantheon Books, 1976), which describes how Washington allows private consultants to make many of its public policy decisions.

7. Mark L. Goldstein, "Spending Spree," *Government Executive* 23, no. 8 (August 1991), p. 9.

8. Mark L. Goldstein, "The Shadow Government," *Government Executive* 22, no. 5 (May 1990), p. 30.

9. Bernard J. Bennington, Board on Telecommunications and Computer Applications, Commission on Engineering and Technical Systems, National Research Council, *Beyond FTS2000* (Washington, D.C., 1989), p. 96.

10. See generally, Office of the Inspector General, Department of Defense, *Audit Report: Contracted Advisory and Assistance Services Contracts*, No. 91-041 (Washington, D.C., February 1, 1991).

11. Ibid.

12. U.S. General Accounting Office, *Government Contractors*, GAO/GGD-92-11 (Washington, D.C., November 1991), p. 3.

13. U.S. Department of Energy, *Organizational Conflicts of Review Panel Report*, January 19, 1990, p. 4.

14. Office of Inspector General, National Aeronautics and Space Administration, *Audit of Fastener Products: Marshall Space Flight Center*, A-MA-88-004 (Washington, D.C., February 2, 1989), p. 8.

15. William Booth, "Hubble Monitors Say They Were Overworked, Overconfident," *The Washington Post*, July 3, 1990, p. A4.

16. Phil Kuntz, "NASA Audit Questioned Fees Paid to Hubble Builders," *Congressional Quarterly*, July 7, 1990, p. 2128.

17. Department of Energy, Memorandum from Berton J. Roth to John C. Tuck (Washington, D.C., October 31, 1989).

18. Mathew L. Wald, "Energy Chief Says Top Aides Lack Skills to Run U.S. Bomb Complex," *The New York Times*, June 28, 1989, p. A1.

19. U.S. Senate, *The Department of Energy's Reliance on Private Contractors*, p. 12.

20. Statement of Dr. Joel S. Hirschorn, senior associate, Office of Technology Assessment, to the Subcommittee on Federal Services, Post Office and Civil Service, Committee on Governmental Affairs, United States Senate, Washington, D.C. February 3, 1989, p. 1.

21. Ibid., p. 3.

22. National Academy of Public Adminstration, *Maintaining the Program Balance: A Report for the National Aeronautics and Space Administration* (Washington, D.C., January 1991), p. viii.

23. Ibid., p. viii–ix.

24. Ibid., p. xii.

25. Ibid., p. x.

26. Donald F. Kettl, Testimony to the Subcommittee on Human Resources, Committee on Post Office and Civil Service, U.S. House of Representatives, Washington, D.C., December 5, 1989, p. 1.

27. Executive Office of the President, *Budget of the United States Government, Fiscal Year 1992* (Washington, D.C.: U.S. Government Printing Office, 1991), Part Seven, p. 132.

28. Council of Economic Advisors, *Economic Report of the President* (Washington, D.C.: U.S. Government Printing Office, 1991), p. 187.

29. Executive Office, *Budget . . . , Fiscal Year 1992*, Part Two, p. 201.

30. Ibid., Part Two, p. 202.

31. Ibid.

32. U.S. General Accounting Office, *Characteristics of Defaulted Borrowers in the Stanford Student Loan Program*, GAO/HRD-91-82BR (Washington, D.C. April 1, 1990), p. 1.

Chapter Seven

1. U.S. Department of Transportation, *National Transportation Strategic Planning Study*, as reported in Office of Technology Assessment, *Delivering the Goods: Public Works Technologies, Management and Financing* (Washington, D.C., April 1991), p. 17.

2. National Council on Public Works Improvement, *Fragile Foundations: A Report on America's Public Works*, February 1988, p. 34.

3. Ibid., p. 37.

4. David Alan Aschauer, *Public Investment and Private Growth: the Economic Benefits of Reducing America's "Third Deficit"* (Washington, D.C.: Economic Policy Institute, 1990), p. 2.

5. Ibid., p. 17.

6. Ibid., p. 15.

7. National Council on Public Works Improvement, *Fragile Foundations*, p. 38.

8. Ibid.

9. Ibid., p. 43.

10. OTA, *Delivering the Goods*, p. 15.

11. Executive Office of the President, *Budget of the United States Government, Fiscal Year 1992* (Washington, D.C.: U.S. Government Printing Office, 1991), Part Seven, p. 88.

12. U.S. General Accounting Office, *Transportation Infrastructure*, GAO/ RCED-90-81B (Washington, D.C., December 1989), p. 39.

13. Mike Mills, "Skinner Steers Federal U-Turn As Interstate Dead Ends," *Congressional Quarterly* 48, no. 50 (December 15, 1990), p. 4134.

14. Don Phillips, "Officials Confront Mysterious, Rapid Rise in N.Y. Air Traffic Delays," *The New York Times*, July 17, 1990. p. A3.

15. U.S. Department of Transportation, Federal Aviation Adminstration, *Airport Capacity Enhancement Plan April 1988*, as reported in OTA, *Delivering the Goods*, p. 121.

16. Ibid., p. 121.

17. Ibid., p. 121.

18. John H. Cushman Jr., "Airports Planning for Big Windfalls," *The New York Times*, November 5, 1990, A14.

19. Executive Office, *Budget . . . , Fiscal Year 1992*, Part Six, p. 13.

20. Ibid.

21. Ibid.

22. OTA, *Delivering the Goods*, p. 170.

23. Ibid.

24. Ibid., p. 171.

25. Ibid., p. 172.

26. Ibid.

27. Robert D. Reischauer, "Fiscal Federalism in the 1980s: Dismantling or Rationalizing the Great Society," in Marshall Kaplan and Peggy Cuciti, eds., *The Great Society and Its Legacy: Twenty Years of U.S. Social Policy* (Durham, N.C.: Duke University Press, 1986), p. 179.

28. Advisory Commission on Intergovernmental Relations, *Significant Features of Fiscal Federalism*, 1988 ed. (Washington, D.C. December 1987), vol. 1, p. 15.

29. U.S. Conference of Mayors, as reported in Gwen Ifill, "Mayors Cite Shrinking Federal Support," *The Washington Post*, January 25, 1991, p. A6.

30. Larry C. Ledebur, *City Fiscal Distress: Structural Demographic and Institutional Causes* (Washington, D.C.: National League of Cities, March 1991), p. 9.

31. As quoted in Gwen Ifill and David S. Broder, "Governors Welcome Bush Plan," *The Washington Post*, February 4, 1991, p. A1.

32. Julie Rovner, "Governors Ask Congress for Relief from Burdensome Medicaid Mandates," *Congressional Quarterly* 49, no. 6 (February 16, 1991), p. 416.

33. Randy Arndt, "NLC Fiscal Survey: Budget Gap on Rise," *Nation's Cities Weekly* 14, no. 27 (July 8, 1991), p. 1.

34. National Governors' Association, *Governors' Weekly Bulletin* 25, no. 16 (April 19, 1991), p. 2.

35. Daniel M. Weintraub, "State Budget Deficit Pegged at $12.6 Billion," *The Los Angeles Times*, March 31, 1991, p. A1.

Chapter Eight

1. The Housing Act of 1949, 42 USC 1441.

2. The Housing and Urban Development Act of 1968, 42 USC 1441 (a).

3. U.S. Senate, HUD/Mod Rehab Investigation Subcommittee of the Committee on Banking, Housing and Urban Affairs, *Final Report and Recommendations* (Washington, D.C.: U.S. Government Printing Office, 1990), p. 34.

4. Morton J. Schussheim, *The Missions and Management of HUD, CRS Report for Congress* (Washington, D.C.: Congressional Research Service, August 16, 1990), p. 4.

5. U.S. Senate, HUD/Mod Rehab Investigation Subcommittee of the Committee on Banking, Housing and Urban Affairs, *The Abuse and Mismanagement of HUD* (Washington, D.C.: 1990), vol. 1. p. 135.

6. Ibid.

7. U.S. Senate, *Final Report*, p. 175.

8. Ibid., p. 82.

9. U.S. Senate, *The Abuse*, p. 490.

10. U.S. Senate, *Final Report*, p. 83.

11. Ibid, p. 175.

12. Ibid., p. 177.

13. Ibid., p. 180.

14. Internal Revenue Service data base, Annual Summary Statistics, passim.

15. Ibid.

16. Statement of Paul L. Posner, Associate Director, Tax Policy and Administration Issues, U.S. General Accounting Office, to the Committee on Governmental Affairs, U.S. Senate (Washington, D.C., August 1. 1990), p. 1.

17. Mary Ellen R. Fise and M. Kristen Rand, *Pennies for Consumer Protection? A Report on the CSPC's 1991 Budget*, Consumer Federation of America and Consumers Union monograph, May 1990, p. 1.

18. Based on CPSC Fiscal 1991 Budget Request as reported in Fise and Rand, Chart I, unnumbered page.

19. Ibid., p. 30.

20. Ibid., p. 34.

21. Michael deCourcy Hinds, "Cries of Poverty in Cradle of Liberty," *The New York Times*, October 14, 1990, p. A1.

22. Ibid.

23. *The Alaska Lands Act: A Broken Promise* (Washington, D.C.: The Wilderness Society, 1990), passim.

24. As reported in John Lancaster, "Parks, Perks and Pork," *The Washington Post*, December 1, 1990, p. A1.

Epilogue

1. See generally, U.S. House of Representatives, Twenty-Second Report by the Committee on Government Operations, *The Peace Corps: Entering* Its *Fourth Decade of Service* (Washington, D.C.: U.S. Government Printing Office, 1990).

Index